Activities to Help Your Family
Play, Work,
& Serve
Together

MAKING
SUMMER
COUNT

Joyce Heinrich
Annette Heinrich LaPlaca

Harold Shaw Publishers
Wheaton, Illinois

ISBN 0-87788-521-4

Cover design and illustration © 1991 by David LaPlaca

Library of Congress Cataloging-in-Publication Data

Heinrich, Joyce.
    Making summer count : activities to help your family play,
work, and serve together / Joyce Heinrich and Annette
Heinrich LaPlaca.
      p.   cm.
    Includes bibliographical references and index.
    ISBN 0-87788-521-4
    1. Family—Religious life. 2. Family recreation. 3. Activity
programs in Christian education. I. LaPlaca, Annette
Heinrich, 1964— . II. Title
BV4526.2.H36 1991
249-dc20
                                   91-11262
                                   CIP

---

99 98 97 96 95 94 93 92 91

10 9 8 7 6 5 4 3 2 1

To Lucille Brock,
our beloved Mother and Grandmother,
who first set the standard
of love and unselfish living
for our family

Contents

A Word from Joyce . . .

It's almost your turn—school will soon be out. And though you may be feeling anxious about the workload that's headed your way, I must confess to having a perspective that's different from yours—I'm glad!

As a teacher I've been working from the proverbial dawn to dark: planning, teaching, grading, figuring percentiles, recording.

For months I've taught the children, retaught them, and re-retaught them!

I've cleaned up after them when they've wet on the floor, bled on their clothes, and thrown up in their desks.

I've nodded droopily while beginning readers plodded . . . at . . . the . . . pace . . . of . . . one . . . word . . . per . . . second.

I've tried to stay poised through electrifying sessions of Show-and-Tell when one never knows what will be shown or told—like the day when one little girl announced, "Last night my cousin's water broke—"

I've sat in paste, had flowers and water dumped on me, had my toenail blackened, and suffered the loss of at least one hundred knee-hi nylons.

I've had to admire (in fact, gasp over dramatically) dead flowers, squished worms, hair braids, inscrutable drawings, loose or missing teeth, and a wide assortment of owies.

I've prayed for my students and with them, worried about them, and agonized over the great burdens some children bear.

In short, I'm tired, and I gladly pass the baton of responsibility back to you for the summer. But with that responsibility I'd like also to pass on some tricks of the trade that I've learned and gathered from friends and experienced teachers over the years.

Teachers know lots of tricks! After all, it's part of the job to come up with creative ways to build interest and teach concepts. Annette and I have attempted to pack this book with some of our best and most workable ideas.

May God give you his guidance and his joy as you become the teacher for the summer.

And a Word from Annette . . .

It's a dog-eat-dog, rat-race kind of world out here for us adults, and now that I'm here in the grown-up world I realize how vastly important those early years of my life were—when I learned to love, learned to work, learned to serve, learned to laugh and enjoy, and learned to know the Savior. Realizing how critical those childhood years can be, my empathies turn toward today's children and young people, and my desire to build their lives spiritually grows stronger day by day.

These were some of my life's proudest moments:

Seeing parents' delighted faces as my two-and-three-year-old class (after excessive blood, sweat, tears, prompting, pulling, and practicing) sang "Kum-Ba-Ya" with hand motions in African costumes they made themselves during the church's missions conference.

Receiving five warm, wet, wonderful good-night smooches from Jon, Greg, Annie, Tommy, and Jenna—with whom I'd hopped, skipped, jumped, sang, laughed, hugged, and prayed all evening, and hearing the soft words in my ear, "You're the best babysitter we've ever had. I love you!"

Wearily watching from my front porch as the last mom picked up the last junior higher from my house late one Saturday morning. "We're not going to let you sleep," the girls from my Sunday school class had warned me—and they didn't. After an evening of pizza and videos, we lay on the carpet all night laughing and talking about what it really means to build friendships and to grow positive, honest relationships with boys.

Opening a letter from a junior higher who had finished reading one of my books for young people: "Your book seemed really real. I think it helped me."

In a world of disintegrating families and multiplied temptations outside the family, children need the building blocks of spiritual ethics more than ever. Kids need to learn to give and receive love; they need to find useful things to do with their hands and to feel the satisfaction of work well done; they need to move outward beyond the encompassing realm of self to see that others have needs and feelings and that they can help; and they need to laugh and play and enjoy as they learn.

And you—the parent—are the primary organizer/caretaker/overseer of your child's summer months. That's what this book is all about. Mom and I want to provide some ideas and tools to help you create a love-filled, learning-filled, fun-filled summer that builds your children's future.

Our prayers go with you!

If I approach summertime with dread, it will be dreadful. However, if I anticipate enjoyment, chances are it will be enjoyable.
GIGI GRAHAM TCHIVIDJIAN

Growing Together in the Family
Section 1

Growing Togetherness

Summer is coming!

After nine long, orderly, organized, predictable months, **school is going to be out.** All of your children will be home 100 percent of the time—and then some!

Not only will *your* children be home, but at least half the neighborhood kids will congregate in your back yard or your family room. It's not enough that you'll have to teach your own children, but now you'll find yourself instructing the neighbors' kids not to swear or tell gross jokes or to go through your cupboards. The cookies and popsicles that were last week's whole supply will now vanish in a day, and your family Band-Aid can will empty overnight.

You'll begin girding up your emotional loins to meet the demands of refereeing fights and squabbles and bickering and the never-ending arguments over game rules.

And you grit your teeth in dread, fearing the first time you'll hear those absolutely maddening words ... "Mom, I'm bored! There isn't anything to do." (This is inevitable and should be included in a category with death and taxes.)

The summer I (Joyce) heard this complaint on the *second* day of vacation was the same summer I borrowed a tactic of Bob's (my husband) and decided that a good offense was my best defense. I had to *do* something with all these children (we had five in a seven-year span)—but what?!

I went to the Lord for help on this practical matter. I asked him for ideas for things to do with Marc, Annette, Dawn, Adele, and Brock during the summer so they wouldn't be bored and so they wouldn't waste those important hours. The Lord answered those requests and—just like our Lord—he did a lot more besides!

During one of my college years at Wheaton, we had an excellent homecoming theme that I've remembered on many occasions since. The theme was "Not Somehow, but Triumphantly." Beginning in early June, the children will be all yours. Annette and I would like to share some ideas with you that have been tried and found to be both fun and valuable for growth. We hope these ideas will help make your summer not a "Somehow" experience—not just a three-month endurance test—but a "Triumphant" one—a lovely, profitable happening for both you and your children. We hope this summer will truly be a significant summer!

If you are willing to invest some time and thought for structuring the coming summer months, you will gain the profit of happier hours, happier children, and a happier you.

Have you ever despaired of your children really loving one another? When bickering or jealousy or tattling rear their ugly heads, you feel as if God's kingdom of love is *never* going to reign in your household. I (Joyce) remember so many times when I cried out to God, "Please, Lord! Please help these children learn to love each other!"

After all, love is utterly basic. It is the foundation of all healthy relationships. 1 Corinthians 13 sums it up pretty well: Without love, nothing matters, nothing is gained. We need to love Jesus and trust his love for us. It's our love for him that should become the basic motivator for service and also the method by which we serve. It is love that causes us to forgive and forget, to see the best in others, to do lovingkindnesses for others. Love is the essential ingredient of family interaction that builds happy and healthy people.

I offer a word of hope: after all these years, my children are *friends*. They really *do* love each other now—and they know how to show it.

So how does family love happen? "Line upon line, precept upon precept," a little here, some there, your example, your guidance, your teaching, your prayers— little by little, children are conformed to Christ's image.

A relationship that is characterized by genuine love and affection is likely to be a healthy one, even though some parental mistakes and errors are inevitable.
DR. JAMES DOBSON

We've devoted the next pages to activities, Scriptures, and devotions that build family unity and love. This summer in the family classroom, each of your children can learn more about the other members of his family and about how he fits into the whole. He can learn more about God's design for the family. We trust that these activity ideas and family devotional ideas will help you adapt your family's summertime fun to include the building blocks of strong family unity in your unique family. Your children will learn more about what it means to be a mom, to be a dad, to be a contributing person in the world. They will consider what it's like to be a considerate brother or a sister, and to step in one another's shoes.

Don't let the number of these ideas overwhelm you. We don't expect you to incorporate *all* of them into your summer plans. Choose one or two, and enjoy! We hope that moms and dads will enjoy the fun as much as the children will.

Learning Activities

Children love to anticipate events—any event. It doesn't have to be awesome or even particularly important. Do you remember how very long a year seemed when you were little? Did you measure the year from Christmas to Christmas—with a birthday in between? Children mark time from event to event—not from date to date as we adults do.

The boredom children experience during the long summer months is at least partially due to a sense of timelessness and aimlessness. During the school months they follow a routine, and daily plans are established for them by teachers and the school schedule. But in the summer months, it's easy to let too many days go by without a purpose, without something to anticipate.

So at the outset of our first significant summer, the children and I (Joyce) together laid out plans for the whole vacation.

We unrolled some white shelf paper and grabbed a marker to set up our three-month calendar. (Ready-made calendars and sticker symbols are available at school-supply centers, if you prefer.) And then we filled in the appropriate squares with every little thing we could think of that would take place during the summer. Because the children were young—some of them pre-readers—it was important to combine symbols and words.

Each Sunday square had a small church drawn on it. "Fun at Church" appeared on each Wednesday square.

The Fourth of July got a little flag. Grandma's and Dad's birthdays were noted with miniature cakes, and of course we marked Labor Day and The First Day of School. We found out the days our church would host boys and girls for Vacation Bible School and also marked the days set aside for our family vacation.

We added new events as the days passed:

Anniversaries
Family adventures and field trips
Little league games
Swim lessons, music lessons
Doctor/dental appointments
Shopping trips for new shoes or school clothes
Friends' visits or visits to friends
Good deed outings
Summer camp

Remembering these events for *all* family members makes even the younger children feel they are important and that they belong. And the visual aid of seeing coming events on the calendar helps preschoolers measure time and know "how long" it will be until "such and such" a happening will take place.

With our calendar up on the wall for all to see and track, the framework for functioning in an enriched environment was in place.

We assigned a part of each morning for work (more about this in the next chapter) and afternoons for fun and friends. We planned at least one—sometimes two—adventures or field trips each week. (Because of this many of the places we always meant to get to but could never find the time to visit were visited at last!) One of the delightful surprises of the summer was that some of the least pretentious plans became the longest remembered.

Adele still reminds me of the afternoon we took shoe-boxes and went into our own back yard to discover and collect nuggets from nature. We put wildflowers, garden flowers, long grass, smooth rocks, sparkly rocks, bird feathers, rabbit fur, pine cones, etc. in the boxes—all the while marveling at God's creative genius and power. The older children mounted their finds in scrapbooks and labeled each item. Adele was just four, but she kept her shoebox of treasures beside her bed for a very long time.

Part of the magic of that experience had to be the holding of hands, the quiet heat of the sun on our backs, the exchange of information and ideas, and the "out loud" praise of a wonderful Creator! Of such stuff are memories made—of such stuff is love strengthened.

All about Me

One ongoing project for this summer could be a personal book for each child in your family, created by that child. Provide a scrapbook (or a photo album or colored paper) for each child. Encourage your child to fill the pages of his or her book with photos or mementos or magazine clippings that reflect his or her uniqueness.

For example, nine-year-old Mike might fill his pages with baby and childhood pictures provided by Mom, a small pennant for his favorite football team, and magazine clippings about skateboarding, his favorite pastime. The book might also include any school awards (either originals or photocopies), any special drawings or story-writing, etc. If Mike dumped a bowl of strawberry ice cream over someone's head when he was two, he might include a magazine photo of ice cream. If he broke his arm the year before, he might make a drawing of himself with a cast and a sling.

When I (Annette) was young, I discovered that Mom had an old-fashioned wooden photo album with my name spelled out in wood letters on the cover. It was filled with my baby pictures. Mom let me remove those photos and make it *my own book* about me. I still have that album—though somewhere along the line (probably in junior high) I once again cleared the pages of the "Annette" book. But it gave me quite a thrill to see my own name on a big book.

The possibilities are as unique as each of your children. When the books are finished, set aside special times (perhaps after the regular family devotional period) to study the books, one each evening or one each week. This is a time when the whole family together demonstrates caring for one of its members by concentrating their attention on him or her. Finish up the hour with prayer, thanking God for the uniqueness of the child and praying for the years to come.

These "All about Me" booklets will be an ongoing source of positive memories and will become a treasure to the future families of your children. Ten years from now, your child may delight to recapture forgotten memories: the time his dog got sprayed by a skunk, the day the orthodontist put on her braces, or the summer everybody took swimming lessons.

For now, your children will learn that who they are is valuable and important to the other members of the family.

> **The sensitive parent observes each child and learns how God designed him.**
> CHARLES SWINDOLL

Lunch with Dad

A friend of ours makes a summer habit of taking her children to visit Dad for lunch now and then. Of course, it is quite likely that many moms will be working as well, and this activity can be adapted for Mom and Mom's lunch hour.

If Dad has an hour lunch break from his work, or if he can get an hour for one special day, pack a lunch and join Dad for the midday meal. Allow the children to help plan the menu and prepare the food. If possible, pack some sort of surprise for Dad—a favorite dessert, short love notes to be read during the rest of the workday, or a small present for his workplace (a homemade paperweight, a framed family picture, or original artwork).

Of course, it can also be fun for the children to "eat where Dad eats." If Dad typically eats lunch in a restaurant, this may be possible only if finances permit. If Dad eats in a cafeteria at his workplace, you may be permitted to bring your packed lunch inside.

This activity reinforces family togetherness by learning more about Dad and his workday and by serving Dad. Children can learn that it is important for them to encourage Dad, who works hard to provide for them.

A Campfire without the Camp

One family we love and admire shares that their favorite family memory was periodic bonfires* and sing-alongs on warm summer evenings. Sometimes it was their own family alone; sometimes extended family and friends were included. The more the merrier!

You just can't find an atmosphere more conducive to building family unity than a campfire. It is the perfect place for banter, sharing the latest jokes, doing skits, or for Grampa to share stories of the old days. It gives the family musicians a chance to shine and provides a legitimate stage for the family ham to do his thing.

Children can enjoy anticipating this time by thinking of the songs they will request at the sing-along. If the

*If your city has a no-burn ordinance, a short trip to a local park will give you a safe and legal place to build your bonfire.

children request a song you do not know, let them teach you. A child feels he is a full participator when he gets a chance to teach the grown-ups.

You may want to end your campfire time with worship songs and a short devotional or time for prayer for your family.

To make each other laugh, to share fun, to sing together is to find joy in one another's company—what a great bonder and builder of family appreciation!

Family Field Trips

The family field trip could be one of your strongest builders of understanding between family members. These trips are designed to focus on one family member at a time to learn more about that person's work or interests. To spark your own ideas for your unique family field trips, we've included a sample of the fictional Finley family—Frank and Frieda and their children, Freddie and Frannie.

Frank Finley (Dad) is a butcher at a local grocery store. For Dad's field trip, Frank and his wife arranged with the manager of the store to give the family a tour. Frieda and the children enjoyed seeing the reverse side of a familiar place—their local grocery store. They walked into enormous freezers, watched stockboys flatten giant boxes by cutting the edges, sampled goodies in the bakery section (where they were amazed to see a big barrel of frosting and got to watch the cake decorator), and—best of all—they toured the back rooms of the meat department, where their father showed them how many sections of meat could come from one cow and how deftly he used large meat cleavers. They were awed by the knives and huge slabs of meat, and they learned a lot about foods they eat every day.

Frieda Finley makes and collects miniatures—tiny replicas of household items and furniture. She and all the family enjoy the doll houses and fancy rooms she decorates—all tiny and proportionally true to size. For her field trip, the whole family went to the local art museum, where there was a visiting display of miniatures. The children realized that Mom's hobby was really a form of art and that many craftsmen and historians used this unique craft to duplicate rooms from the homes of famous people and various periods of history.

Freddie's hobby is star-gazing. His room is full of constellation charts and posters of "Star Trek" and "Star Wars" movies. He has his own telescope, which he uses to see the stars on clear nights. For Freddie's field trip, the whole family went to the Planetarium, where they all learned a lot about the solar system, the galaxy, and the constellations. To top off the day's fun, they made pizza and rented "Star Wars" to watch on their VCR.

Frannie Finley likes to draw, to paint, to construct. She is the artist of the family. For Frannie's field trip, the whole family visited the Children's Art Museum located in the basement of their local art museum. Each of them got to help paint a large mural, and they enjoyed the various hands-on displays about color, shapes, and perspective.

From these examples, you get the idea! Each of these activities would be fun for *any* family—and you might want to plan field trips to the grocery store, to the planetarium, to a miniatures shop or display, and to the art museum. But these field trips were uniquely tailored for the Finley family's interests.

If your child loves to read, locate the nearest book publisher or book printer and ask if someone could take your family on a tour to show how books are created and produced and distributed. If your hobby is coin collecting, find out about visiting a mint or a large bank, where your child could hold a new coin or a thousand-dollar bill right in his hand.

When I (Annette) was a girl, my school class took a field trip to the factory where Tonka toys were built. Almost any child would be fascinated to see how toy trucks and cars are mass produced, painted, and warehoused.

These field trips are an occasion to let your imagination run wild. Some ordinary trips—like the grocery store—afford interesting and enjoyable learning experiences for your child. Don't be afraid to contact business people for a field trip favor. Most of them will respond positively to helping young people learn. Your own co-workers or those of your husband should be particularly interested in contributing something to your family.

These trips tell each member of your family that his or her interests are important to all of you and offer excellent opportunities to broaden a child's experiences and his understanding of various occupations or hobbies.

> **God has woven certain
> characteristics into the inner fabric
> of every child, giving him his physical
> features, emotions, basic personality,
> interests, and abilities.**
> CHARLES SWINDOLL

Personalized Bulletin Boards

A large bulletin board (or a large section of cork board) can afford more personalized family fun and further highlight talents and interests.

When I (Annette) was young, my sisters and I had a long classroom-sized bulletin board in our bedroom. Mom went to lots of trouble to make us fantastic bulletin boards that were the envy of all our neighborhood playmates. I remember specifically one about Hawaii, with large cut-out Hawaiian children, palm trees, and sunshine, and another with a yellow background, a long bright rainbow, and a pot of gold.

You and your children could spend a rainy day or two designing your own bulletin boards. For example, Freddie Finley would want to create a bulletin board full of stars in constellations. You might use strips of green crepe paper, twisted from top to bottom (seaweed), against a blue background to make an "Under the Sea" bulletin board. You and the children could make construction paper or tissue paper fish and ocean plants. Or let your imagination run and add deep-sea divers, sunken ships, and treasure.

Another idea is to select a certain country—maybe one where you have relatives or missionary friends—and cut out magazine pictures to show the culture, foods, and landscape of that country. The background might be the shape of the country or a map of the country.

The ideas for your bulletin boards are as varied as your creativity. Be sure to let your children brainstorm for ideas, and allow them to change the bulletin board every couple of weeks (or every rainy day!).

Saturday Afternoon Adventures

When our family was young, Dad would occasionally rescue Mom (Joyce) on a Saturday afternoon by removing all of us children from the house so she could get a nap or a long bath (or, more likely, catch up on housework).

Such memorable adventures they were! Dad took us to the top of the tallest building in Minnesota. He took us on a tour of the capitol building, where we climbed a long, narrow stairway up to the dome-shaped top and reached out to touch the giant golden horses that ornament the building. We rode a city bus—something we seldom did. Dad took us on a long, long hike, during which we all got lost, got stuck in some squishy, quicksand-like dirt, and ruined our clothes (beyond even Mom's hope of repair).

These were good opportunities for Mom to have some personal time. During the long years and months and days of the demands of childcare, those few hours must have been much-needed and very precious. And even more importantly, they were great opportunities for us to have fun—the learning kind of fun—with Dad.

If you are a single parent, you may not have the option of a spouse who can "rescue" you for a few hours on a Saturday. Don't be afraid to ask your child's uncle or grandfather or cousin to do a favor like this for you. At worst he can beg off because of a busy schedule. At best you offer your children some time with another adult and you offer your relative an opportunity to enjoy your delightful children.

Family Figures
If you have a large wall that is relatively free for displaying artwork, you might want to fill it with the life-size figures of your family.

Using large butcher paper, trace each family member's figure—from head to toe while lying down on the paper. Each member can draw himself—with his own hair and eye colors and his favorite clothes. Or choose partners to draw each other; this exercise builds awareness of other family members. Put your family up against the wall together (even if it is the garage wall).

One warning: Unless your cat is de-clawed, we don't recommend tracing pets!

Reading Aloud Together
How often have you read a book and then handed it immediately to your best friend? It draws people together as friends to read and enjoy the same book. Your children will benefit from times of reading aloud together as a family. This is a good time for older children to practice their read-aloud skills or an excel-

lent time for Dad to spend some time with the children when he is home from work.

Take a moment to consider how your ability to read well has broadened you personally. Books are a wonderful way to share as a family. Allow each family member to choose a book for group reading, then work your way together through the stack during the summer. An excellent resource for selecting fiction books for your family reading is *How to Grow a Young Reader* by John and Kathryn Lindskoog (Shaw, 1989). We have also included a list of some suggested favorites at the end of this book.

Some of our family favorites for out-loud reading are: the *Little House on the Prairie* series for young readers; the *Anne of Green Gables* series for middlers; and the George MacDonald translations for teens. Some George MacDonald fans whom we know traveled to Scotland for a family vacation to find and visit the places they have grown to love through these books.

Be sure to visit and use your church and public libraries during the summer. Most public libraries offer summer story hours, and many churches have summer reading contests, complete with certificates of achievement. (This is an idea you might adapt for home use by creating your own award certificates.)

A Family Production

The Heinrich family is becoming rather well known for its fun and sometimes ridiculous "shows" or "plays."

I (Annette) remember enacting the Christmas story with the whole family when there were only four of us. Mom (Joyce) was the angel who brought the "good tidings of great joy," and I was Mary. Since Marc was Joseph, Dad had to play the part of all three wise men!

We have a family snapshot of a murder mystery written, directed, and produced—complete with a musical finish—by the Heinrich children (Annette and siblings), then ages five to twelve. The story was complete with a villain, an elderly millionaire with a box full of jewels, a maid, a gardener, and a very young sheriff.

Since then we have put together silly plays and productions for special occasions: wedding anniversaries and wedding receptions and, most recently, our Granny's eightieth birthday. These very limited (in props, in actors, in talent, in everything!) productions have been reenactments of important events in the lives of our family members.

For a special occasion this summer (or just for fun), put together a light-hearted reenactment of an important family event. This might be the way Mom and Dad met and fell in love, or when the first baby was born, or some adventure the family shared on a vacation or when moving. Be sure to put your heads together with your children's to brainstorm ideas. If your children are older, plant the idea and let them run with it. They'll enjoy the hours of laughing and practicing.

You may want to select a certain audience for your production. The kids may put it on for parents, or you may want to invite extended family members. For further fun, allow children to create construction paper programs and bake refreshments.

Family Shirts

Our friend Carol recommends family t-shirts. These could be regular printed t-shirts, one for each member of the family. Or, your family could come up with a family logo and have special t-shirts printed just for you.

An alternative to having t-shirts printed would be using the washable, permanent bright-colored fabric paints, puff paints, and sparkle paints now easily available in any craft center. Each family member could design and paint his own shirt.

Having a matched set of t-shirts is a fun way to say, "We're a team. We're in it together!" And if your summer includes an extended family reunion, print t-shirts for everyone!

Family Projects

Like the family field trips, creative family-personalized group projects can be another learning and enjoyable activity for your family. We'll look to the fictional Finleys again for examples.

Since Frank Finley is a butcher, Frieda and the children used a large piece of white shelf paper (or a piece of butcher paper) to draw a large cow, and then they separated the segments to show where the butcher would cut. They labeled the sections with the names of the cut of meat—"rump roast," "ribs," etc. They presented Bossy the Cow to Dad as a surprise.

Frieda and the children used a box and attempted to recreate their own living room in miniatures. This involved painting the "walls" of the box, securing a carpet scrap for the floor, and creating light cardboard and construction paper paintings and items of furniture.

For Freddie, they used wire hangers and styrofoam balls to construct a solar system. They used the children's paints to give the planets bright colors. This project required a bit of research in the library's encyclopedias.

For Frannie, they used clay to make mini-figurines of the family. Frannie, who showed the most talent, did the detail work on the faces.

I (Annette) remember my brother Marc building a replica of the city we lived in on a large wooden board. We were all fascinated by this project, with its painted streets and tiny trees and telephone wires. No doubt Marc learned a lot about all the things that make up a city—from residential neighborhoods to business zoning to electrical and water plants.

Another time Marc glued safety matches—with the heads up—to a board in the shape of the United States. After dark on the fourth of July, he lit up the whole United States. The flash of flame was impressive and made a wonderful new kind of "fireworks!"

More than once, Mom (Joyce) helped me re-wallpaper and carpet my dollhouse using pages from an old wallpaper sample book and carpet scraps.

A dear family friend helped Adele cut, sew, and stuff a throw pillow for her bed.

Let your children make project suggestions. They might come up with some outlandish ideas, but you might be able to adapt them into a workable summer project. Exercise your own creativity as you help your children exercise theirs.

Play-dough Grab-bag

Our friend Carol suggests an activity that is especially helpful to little ones who have a hard time keeping their busy hands still during family devotions.

Each member of the family will receive a lump of play dough and a slip of paper at the beginning of the devotional time. The little note tells them what objects—objects found in the passage or story being studied—they are to mold during the reading. At Christmas time, the figures might make up a nativity scene. At Easter, they might be a crown of thorns, a cross, and a tomb. For the Feeding of the 5,000, your family might mold a boy, a basket, bread, fish, etc. The activity illustrates the Bible text in a way that is both fun and memorable.

You and your children might want to make your own play dough right at home, so we've included the recipe Mom (Joyce) and our Aunt Konnie use at preschool.

Small World School Play Dough

4 cups flour	3½ cups boiling water
1 cup salt	⅓ cup cold oil
4 Tbs alum	food coloring

Mix well. Knead while hot. The dough will be sticky at first, but it becomes workable. Store in an air-tight container.

Devotional Suggestions

Regular Family Devotions

With mandatory "sit and be quiet" times at a minimum, summer provides the perfect opportunity to establish the habit of family devotions. Devotion time might be set aside for thoughtful and tender exchange of ideas and reactions to God's Word, or another time it might be a joyous (maybe even a bit raucous!) skit designed to teach principles or to reenact a Bible story. Whatever the mood or theme, a family devotional time builds togetherness and unity between family members and with the Lord Jesus Christ.

Our friend Carol has two children who are nearly grown now; both Shari and Dan are in college. But Carol tells us that one of her children's fondest memories is of their family's regular devotions.

Carol and Jim set down two easy-to-follow guidelines for their family devotions: each person must bring his own Bible, and each must contribute something during the devotional period. These two guidelines reinforced two important truths about studying God's Word: that Bible study is personal discovery and that Bible study is active rather than passive.

Shari and Dan offered simple questions or basic observations about the Scripture passage being studied, and Carol's and Jim's positive guidance and encouragement taught them that believers can learn from one another in a group and that the Bible is full of truths to discover. Requiring each child to contribute a question or comment ensures age-appropriate devotions. It also gives the children an opportunity to ask questions about things they don't understand or to learn by the application of Scripture to their particular interests or problems.

A delightful Brazilian family with three preschool boys stayed with us for a week. Each morning after breakfast the mother would gather her little team around our children's play table. She read a short Scripture passage and then asked her boys questions. She let them ask her questions. They sang some peppy choruses and songs with gusto and clapping (all in Portuguese, of course), and then they would ask Jesus for help through prayer for many practical needs pertaining to their lives. What a priority this mother set on training her children! Even on vacation with no other props or tools than a Bible, she had pertinent and enjoyable teaching for her sons.

You will have to use your own judgment and your own knowledge of family schedule and family attention spans to determine when and how often your family will hold a devotional period. Preschoolers generally won't last longer than fifteen minutes. For children of elementary school ages, time your devotions for twenty-thirty minutes, depending on their ages and the number of people in your family. Twenty-thirty minutes is also a good length for family devotions with your teenagers.

When there is a wide spread in the ages of your children, special problems present themselves: For which age group do you select material? How long should the devotions be? And *how* do you keep everyone interested?

You'll have to experiment with different approaches to discover what works for your family. If there is a marked age difference—for example, two preschoolers and two junior-highers—then two sets of devotions may be in order. But we rather favor having one whole family devotional time, as this provides the additional benefit of teaching the children consideration of the others' needs and interests and patience in waiting for their own needs to be addressed.

So you might provide a short devotional for each age group and sing songs that all know and enjoy . . .

Or you could alternate age-appropriate material targeting one group one time and the other the next . . .

Or perhaps you'll find that Carol's and Jim's format adequately covers the age-spread in your family.

There are many excellent books available on conducting family devotions. Check out your local Christian bookstore or your church library. Children's Bibles, Bible storybooks, flannelgraphs, and devotional books designed for various age groups are abundant and will provide you with good resources.

**To be successful parents,
we must first love the Word of God.**
GEORGE SWEETING

Building Family Togetherness

■ Devotion #1: Brothers and Sisters

Over the course of a week or two, read and discuss the story of the brothers Jacob and Esau and their problems. Be sure to include the story of the reconciliation of the two men as adults.

Important Scripture Passages
Genesis 25:19-34
Genesis 27:1—28:9
Genesis 28:10—31:55
Genesis 32:1-21; 33:1-11

Wrapping It Up
The following devotional might be helpful in summarizing your Scripture reading of the past week, especially if your children are preschool and lower elementary-school aged.

Jack and Jackie's Happy Day

Jack and Jackie held tight to Mom's hands. The twins were four years old and big enough to go to Happy Day Preschool.

School *was* a happy place just filled with paints and glue and markers and trucks and blocks and dolls and games. Best of all there were smiling teachers to read stories, put out the snacks, and teach new songs!

Jack and Jackie had already visited their new school, but today was the day they would stay without Mom.

Without Mom? Jack kissed Mom good-bye and dashed off to build with blocks and find a new friend. Jackie kissed Mom, too, but she did not want Mom to go. When their car drove away, a big sadness filled her up until tears began to squeeze out of her brown eyes. She wanted to go home. She wanted her mother.

The teachers came to Jackie with hugs and kind words. But they couldn't help her. Jackie cried louder than ever. Some boys and girls came to pat her back, but that didn't help either. She kept crying big tears.

Jack could hear Jackie crying from the block corner. But he had built a tower as high as his nose, and he did not want to stop to help her. He did not want to stop, but Jackie's crying was making him feel sad inside, too. Jack put the blocks away and sat down at the table beside his sister.

"Jackie," he asked, piling up a big lump of yellow play dough in front of them, "would you like a rolling pin to use on this play dough?"

"No," said Jackie, looking at him with teary eyes. "I want Mommy. I want to go home."

"I know, Jackie. I know you want Mom. Would you like to use this cookie cutter to make a play-dough cookie?"

"No," said Jackie again, crying more quietly now. "I want to see Mommy. I feel tired. I want to go to bed."

"She'll come get us, Jackie, as soon as school is over. She'll come pick us up. Here, Jackie. Try these scissors on the play dough. They really cut it nice!"

Jackie took the scissors and began to cut little play-dough French fries. She lined them up in a row.

"This is fun, Jack," she said. And she let a small smile peep out.

"Look, Jackie!" called Jack. "A big box with bowls and scoops and seeds! Let's try that!"

Soon all of Jackie's tears stopped. Big smiles popped out on both Jack's and Jackie's faces as they shoveled and scooped the seeds. Now Happy Day Preschool really was a happy place for both Jack *and* Jackie!

Questions to answer and talk about:
Do you think Jackie acted like a baby because she cried? Why or why not?

Why did Jack stop building to help Jackie?

Do you think it was Jack's job to help his sister?

Why could Jack help Jackie when the teachers and the other children could not help?

———

This devotional might be helpful in summarizing your Scripture reading of the past week if your children are older elementary or junior high aged.

A Dirty Trick—and How It Turned Out

Once upon a time there was a young man who was a mama's boy and a stinker. Until the Lord straightened him out, Jacob was a real creep. Not only did he cheat his twin brother out of his inheritance, but—with a little help from Mom—he stole his brother's blessing, too. Finally Esau got mad enough to kill. So Jacob hot-footed it out of town, and the brothers didn't see each other for a long, long time.

Twenty years later, the Lord told Jacob to move back to his hometown. Jacob had learned to honor and obey the Lord, so he started making plans. One thing bothered him, though. What if Esau still wanted to break Jacob's neck for the rotten things he had done while they were young? So he sent messengers with all kinds of presents to butter up Esau a little before they met face to face.

No Hard Feelings

But those long years of separation had been good ones for Esau. He'd become wealthy even without the inheritance he'd lost. He'd learned to honor God. And he'd missed his brother.

So the reunion that Jacob dreaded turned out to be a wonderful day for two brothers. Maybe Jacob and Esau sat down together and talked about the years of friendship they'd lost because they allowed favoritism, unforgiveness, and a few dirty tricks to come between them. Now that each brother knew where he stood in relationship to God, the problems of their early life became water under the bridge. (Read their story in Genesis 25:23-34; 27:1–33:20.)

Save Time—Be Friends Now

Hopefully, you and the other members of your family will never have to repair damage as painful as the problems between the brothers Jacob and Esau.

Don't wait twenty years to show your love and forgiveness to one another. Jacob and Esau wasted a lot of years—when they could've been the best of friends. Practice loving and forgiving in your family.

Above all, love each other deeply, because love covers over a multitude of sins. 1 Peter 4:8

Maybe you have a "wound" from a family battle or a family disappointment. Can you trust the Lord to put forgiveness where there is resentment, and a renewed love where there is bitterness?

Maybe you have hurt someone in your family. Ask the Lord to give you courage to say, "I'm sorry," and to make things right between you.*

■ Devotion #2: Loving One Another

Loving one another is so important that the command is repeated over and over by the writers of the books of the New Testament. Over several devotional sessions, look up these references about loving and discuss them, remembering that the first place we have opportunity to show love is right at home.

If your children are ready to use reference resources, you might demonstrate the use of the concordance by sending them on a "Love Hunt"—a search for these and other commands to love one another.

Important Scripture Passages

Matthew 22:37-39;	Philippians 2:2-4
Mark 12:29-31	Colossians 3:12-14
John 13:34-35; 15:12-13, 17	1 Thessalonians 3:12-13
Romans 12:9-10	1 Thessalonians 4:9-10
Romans 13:9-10	1 Timothy 1:5
1 Corinthians 13:1-3	1 Peter 1:22
1 Corinthians 13:4-8a, 13	1 Peter 3:8, 4:8
1 Corinthians 16:14	1 John 3:10-11, 14-18
Galatians 5:14	1 John 4:7-12, 16-21
Ephesians 5:1-2	2 John 5-6

Wrapping It Up

The following devotional might be helpful in summarizing your Scripture reading of the past weeks, especially

*Adapted from Annette Heinrich, Not a Hollywood Family, Shaw, 1989.

if your children are preschool and lower elementary-school aged.

Vangie's Granny

Vangie pushed her ruffled sock into her shiny new shoe and stuck the straps together.

"I'm so happy, I'm so happy," she sang. "I'm so happy, happy, happy, happy, happy, happy, happy!"

Vangie danced a little dance and said out loud, "Granny's coming! Granny's coming!"

She reached into her drawer to find the small silver cross her Grandma had sent her for Christmas. She would wear it to the airport. Vangie's granny lived in a far-away state, but she was flying in for a visit that very day.

I like Granny's smile, thought Vangie. *She smiles at me lots of times. And I like my granny's eyes. They shine when we look at each other. Granny's arms are warm,* she thought. *I like to hug my Granny!*

Vangie remembered Granny's last visit. *Maybe it will be like that again,* she thought. *Maybe we will read stories—like before. We might bake oatmeal cookies, too. Maybe we will take Hot Shot Dog for a walk again. We might swing at the schoolground, just like the last time!*

"I'm so happy, I'm so happy," Vangie sang again.

Vangie scratched Hot Shot Dog behind the ears as they rode in the van. It seemed like it took a long time for Dad to drive all the way to the airport.

Vangie did another dance while she waited for the passengers to get off the plane. Then she saw her own dear Granny!

Vangie's feet almost flew over the tile floor. She jumped into her Granny's arms and kissed and kissed her face.

"Granny," she said between hugs and loves, "do you know why I am kissing you?"

"Why, Vangie?" asked Granny.
"Because, Granny, I love you!"

Questions to answer and talk about:
Why did Vangie love her Granny?
How did Vangie show she loved her Granny?
Are there other ways to show love? Name some.

———

This devotional might be helpful in summarizing your Scripture reading of the past week if your children are older elementary or junior high aged.

Summer Vacation

When Carrie's older sister, Meg, came home from college the summer after her freshman year, Carrie was shocked. Meg was so different! *Whatever it is they did to her at college,* Carrie thought, *I like it!*

Instead of spreading her piles of junk beyond her half of the room and onto Carrie's side, Meg apologized for being such a slob all the time and promised to work at keeping it clean.

Instead of making Carrie grovel before loaning her any clothes, Meg offered them. And she made a big deal of helping Carrie get dressed and fix her hair before a date.

Instead of ignoring her sister to go shopping with her college friends, Meg actually invited Carrie to come along. "We won't tell them how old you are!" she laughed.

Instead of bragging about all her college-life freedoms and privileges, she listened to Carrie talk about high school, struggles with Dad, and hopes for the future.

Carrie couldn't believe the change in Meg!

What Happened to You?

Finally Carrie had to ask, "What happened to make you so different, Meg?"

You can probably guess Meg's answer. She'd met a lot of Christian students at college, and eventually she'd met Christ, too.

Carrie's mouth dropped open in surprise when she saw Meg take a blue Bible out from under her pillow. Meg opened the book to a passage she had marked:

Love is patient, love is kind. It does not envy, it does not boast, it is not proud. 1 Corinthians 13:4

Carrie read the words and nodded. *Yep—those words describe the new Meg,* she thought. *Maybe this Christianity stuff is for real.*

The Love Factor

Meg's loving behavior in her life at home could be an important factor for introducing Carrie to God's love. Her behavior was so different, Carrie had to ask, "What happened to you?"

Does your love give evidence of Christ living in you? Do you think your family members credit your loving actions to your status as a child of God?

Ask God now to give you a faithful love that reminds people—especially those people who live at your house!—of his Son.*

■ Devotion #3: Forgiving in the Family

The story of the life of Joseph is an exciting one for young people. Like all good storytelling, it has strong plot and good character development. When you read the story together as a family over the course of two or three

Adapted from Annette Heinrich, Not a Hollywood Family, *Shaw, 1989.*

weeks, you will discover that Joseph models many of the characteristics you seek to build in yourself and in your children: faithfulness, fervency in prayer, obedience to God, forgiveness, and love for other family members. Your children will also hear the testimony of God's care and provision for Joseph. Especially emphasize the difficulty of Joseph's ambush by his brothers and his willingness later to be forgiving and to see the big picture.

Important Scripture Passages

Genesis 37:1-36	Genesis 42:1-38
Genesis 39:1-23	Genesis 43:1-34
Genesis 40:1-23	Genesis 44:1-34
Genesis 41:1-40	Genesis 45:1-28
Genesis 41:41-57	Genesis 46:1-7, 26-30

Wrapping It Up

The following devotional might be helpful in summarizing your Scripture reading of the past weeks, especially if your children are preschool and lower elementary-school aged.

Tell It to the Tattle Tree

Once upon a time there was a jolly family of seven with a jolly father, a jolly mother, and five jolly children. Well, it must be told that they were jolly some of the time. But there were some times when one brother would get angry at another brother, or when one sister would fight with the other sister. And then—someone would tattle to Mother.

"Mom, he rode my bike without asking!"

"Mom, she said she would do the dishes and now she won't!"

"Mom, he's hogging more than his share of the popcorn!"

"Mom, I can't find my bracelet—she has it, I know!"

And at those times, Mom would clap her hands over her ears.

"It hurts my ears to hear your tattling," she said. "It hurts my heart to hear unkind words. Don't tattle to me any more, children. Go tell it to the Tattle Tree." Mother pointed to the huge and quiet tree that grew by their patio.

So out they went—each brother and each sister shouting their tattles at the Tattle Tree. Mom felt jolly again because her ears and heart did not hurt anymore.

But what do you think happened to the Tattle Tree? A brother watched one of the leaves fall, then another and another—long before Autumn ever came. And a sister saw its branches begin to droop closer and closer to the ground. Then they all noticed that the chickadees no longer chirped in the Tattle Tree, and the sparrows sped away to feed at the neighbor's bird feeder.

"This is sad. This is very sad," they all said. And then no one in the family was jolly at all.

But the father was very wise.

"Perhaps," he told his children, "perhaps if unkind words are killing our tree, then perhaps—just perhaps—kind words will make it healthy and strong again."

"We'll try it," said the children. They began to tattle kind words.

"Tattle Tree, my sister helped me pick up toys today."

"My brother found my missing dime, Tattle Tree, and put it in my pocket!"

"My dad glued the broken bench today, Tattle Tree!"

The loving tattles and kind words floated up and around the sad and sickly tree. Everyone watched and held their breath. Would the leaves stop falling? Sure enough, they did! Would the branches spring back? Sure enough, they did! Would all the birds come back to eat and live in their Tattle Tree again? Sure enough, they did!

The whole jolly family joined hands around the Tattle Tree and hugged hard. Even the Tattle Tree was jolly then and still is—to this very day!

(This is a make-believe story, but it teaches real lessons.)

Questions to answer and talk about:
The Bible says that "tattling separates friends." Are your brothers and sisters your friends?
Why did the jolly mother's heart hurt her when her children tattled?
How do you feel when someone tattles on you?
When something happens in your family that isn't fair, how can it be made right without tattling?

This devotional might be helpful in summarizing your Scripture reading of the past week if your children are older elementary or junior high aged.

Lifetime Guarantee

My family moved about twelve times during the years before I went away to college. In each new place we made good friends, but it took awhile. So every time we moved I thanked God that I had brothers and sisters. It gave me someone to play with or hang out with until I made some friends.

I didn't think about my brothers and sisters in the same category as my friends—you probably don't either. But one day when I started to think about it, I realized, "Hey—I like these people. I bet I'd even like them if they weren't in my family and I'd just met them at school!" It was a great discovery.

Friends Forever
Hopefully, during your lifetime you will make some friends who are true blue—the kind of friends who will stick by you until you're in the old folks' home together, playing shuffleboard and talking about old times. But many of your friendships won't last that long—for lots of different reasons. Maybe your values and personality will change. Maybe your friend's will. Maybe you'll go away to college and never move back to your home state. Or maybe your friend will move. Maybe you'll have six kids someday, and your best friend will be jetsetting around the world in an absorbing career. There's no telling. It's exciting to wonder how our lives and friendships will unfold.

But no matter what other things change, your flesh-and-blood family will always be *your family*. The friendships you develop with your brothers and sisters are lifetime-guarantee friendships.

It Makes a Difference
It makes a difference to think about your family members as forever friends. In the middle of your next fight over a TV program, watch what you say! Ten years down the road, you may not remember what the fight was about, but you'll remember the hurtful words you spoke to one another.

Maybe knowing that your sister or brother is going to be your lifelong friend will make you want to work at that friendship more. Look for the things you like about your brother. Once in a while, go to the mall with your sister instead of your best friend. Invest some time and energy into that long-lasting friendship.

How good and pleasant it is when brothers live together in unity! Psalm 133:1

We love because he first loved us. If anyone says, "I love God," yet hates his brother, he is a liar. For anyone who does not love his brother, whom he has seen, cannot love God, whom he has not seen. And he has given us this command: Whoever loves God must also love his brother. 1 John 4:19-21

Self-Check

What about you? Do your actions and attitudes at home demonstrate your lifetime-guarantee friendship to your brothers and sisters? What are two practical ways you can show your love to a sister or brother today? Ask God to give you creative ideas for building friendships in your family. Ask him to fill you up with his love for your brothers and sisters so that you will be the best possible friend to them.*

■ Devotion #4: God's Family

Your family is unique. When God hand-picked your one-of-a-kind spouse and your one-of-a-kind children, he gave you the bond of family. If the members of your family are Christians, you share another bond—as brothers and sisters in God's own family. Use the following Scriptures to focus on your family's status as God's children.

Important Scripture Passages

Deuteronomy 14:1-2	2 Corinthians 6:16
Jeremiah 32:38-40	1 Peter 2:9-10
John 1:12	1 John 3:1-2
Romans 8:15b-17	

*Adapted from Annette Heinrich, Not a Hollywood Family, *Shaw, 1989.*

Wrapping It Up
The following devotional might be helpful in summarizing your Scripture reading of the past weeks, especially if your children are preschool and lower elementary-school aged.

So Does God

When you open up the Bible you will see that there are lots and lots of pages that tell about Jesus, our God.

Some pages have stories that tell how Jesus was the best kind of doctor because he made sick and hurt people well. Other pages tell what a great teacher Jesus was. His stories were so exciting and his teaching so interesting that people would walk from far away just to hear him talk.

But my favorite pages in the Bible tell us that God is our Father and we are his children. Everyone who believes in Jesus is in God's beloved family.

It is a Father's job to take good care of his children.

Does a good dad get food for his family? So does God!

Does a good dad keep his family safe? So does God!

Does a good dad teach his children all they need to know? So does God!

Does a good dad pray for his children? So does God!

Does a good dad show he loves his children? So does God!

Does a good dad sometimes give gifts to his children? So does God!

God is a Father who will always love us and never leave us. He will be our kind Father until we are grown-up men and ladies and even until we are grandpas and grandmas with gray hair!

When life is over he will take us to his own home in heaven. We will be very happy with our big forever family and our heavenly Father. We will never have to say good-bye to this loving Father God!

Questions to answer and talk about:
How has God given our family food?
How does God teach us?
Has God given us any presents? What are they?
What do you think heaven is like?
What will you do there?
Who will you see?
What will you see?

———

This devotional might be helpful in summarizing your Scripture reading of the past week if your children are older elementary or junior high aged.

The Last Family Reunion

When was the last time you thought about heaven? Did you think about mansions, angels with harps, and streets of gold? What are your most awesome imaginings of heaven?

My family moved about a million times when I was young. (O.K.—it wasn't really that many, but sometimes it seemed like it!) And in every place we found a good church, and we made great friends. I don't write to all of those people, but I often think about them and wish we could be together again.

I don't live close to all the members of my family, either, and often I get a great big longing to see their faces instead of just talking on the phone or waiting for a vacation or for a holiday.

So it's not surprising that the picture of heaven I had when I was young was that of a giant neighborhood full of all the people I've known and loved—all living in one place close enough for me to be with them.

Face to Face

But think how it will be when we see the Lord Jesus face to face! All the frights and stresses and disappointments of the world will be gone forever, and our love for him will multiply by hundreds and hundreds in those first moments when we meet Christ's eyes.

The light of God's glory will fill the place where we, all the members of God's family, are gathered to worship. And the heavenly musicians will play fantastic music we've never heard before, music invented just for honoring God.

The Perfect Family

There, at the last great, eternal Family Reunion, we'll become the perfect family. We'll be perfectly united in worshipping God, our Maker and Creator and true Parent. We won't remember the struggles to communicate with each other and forgive one another. We'll be transformed into Christ's likeness, and we'll finally be like him.

Look forward to that day! Think of it as often as you can, because remembering that you're going to live forever with God changes the way you live from day to day here on earth. Praise God now, in advance, for that great day when we will see the Lord Jesus face to face in the splendid light of his glory.

> *Yet to all who received him, to those who believed in his name, he gave the right to become children of God. John 1:12*
>
> *And by him we cry, "Abba, Father." The Spirit himself testifies with our spirit that we are*

God's children. Now if we are children, then we are heirs—heirs of God and co-heirs with Christ, if indeed we share in his sufferings in order that we may also share in his glory.
Romans 8:15-17

How great is the love the Father has lavished on us, that we should be called children of God!
1 John 3:1*

*Adapted from Annette Heinrich, Not a Hollywood Family, *Shaw, 1989.*

Heigh Ho,
It's Off to Work We Go
Section 2

Working Together

One of the greatest desires children have is to grow up to be like Mom and Dad. Each new skill they learn, each new place they experience, each new phrase or word they define is a building block to maturity, and children instinctively know it.

Work skills are very important to a child's sense of confidence, of accomplishment, and of self-reliance. Mastering the basics of housekeeping and gardening builds a healthy pride and a mindset that says, "I know how to do it!"

When Brock was very young, he struggled with the logistics of hanging his jacket on the hook at preschool using the little strap provided for that purpose. His preschool teacher overheard him muttering under his breath, "I think I can, I think I can, I think I can." And indeed he could!

That's the confidence we want to build. And when children use the skills they know for the comfort and welfare of the family, it also helps them know they are valuable members of the unit—they are needed and wanted. *They belong.*

And let's face it! If you are a working mom or the mother of many, you run through life with chaos yapping at your heels. You can *use* their help. And they need lessons in assuming responsibility, completing a task, and setting priority on assigned responsibility.

So, during the summer weeks, I would make out a job list each day and we would tackle those right away.

Some tasks, like making their own beds and picking up their rooms, were not included on the list, as the children knew they were accountable for those jobs daily. Each day I'd set a target time for finishing our work, usually about 10:00 or 10:30 A.M. The children knew that the remaining time was theirs—for fun and friends.

A good laugh is sunshine in a house.
THACKERAY

Spoonful of Sugar

You probably remember Mary Poppins and her Spoonful of Sugar. "You find the fun, and SNAP! the job's a game!" she sang.

The wise mother takes that Poppins formula and puts it to work for summertime tasks—before the jobs begin, while the family works, and after the work is done.

Before You Begin

1. Vary the tasks assigned. This relieves boredom and ensures that each child learns to do all the jobs.

2. Once in a while, assign the tasks in creative ways. You might cut up the job list and mix the tasks in a hat or a box. Let the children choose their chore from the box. Or, play a form of "Pin the Tail on the Donkey." Blindfolded, the children must point to a spot on the job list, and that's their job for the morning. Or, do a Treasure Hunt. Write the jobs on slips of paper and hide them; each child hunts until he has found his job.

3. Occasionally remind your children WHY you do housework. Be sure your children hear your rationale from time to time about why in the world anyone cleans the house at all! This doesn't have to be delivered as a lecture; in fact, it's best to let the ideas drop here and there as you are reminded of them.

For example, when the job is done say, "The house looks so beautiful when it's shiny and neat, doesn't it?

It reminds me of a pretty picture!" Or, "Whew! I'm sure thankful you carried all that trash out of here, Brock. Can you imagine what our house would smell like if nobody did it?" Or how about, "One reason we're so healthy around here this year must be that we're keeping the toilets and sinks so clean."

You might also point out that doing jobs on schedule avoids "panic pick-up" when guests arrive, and putting things in their places prevents accidents and hunting for lost items.

Whistle While You Work

Mary Poppins would also say, "Well begun is half done!" But, oh! That other half can be pretty important as well.

1. Provide a surprise encouragement treat. Carry a pocket full of M & Ms or gummy bears or chocolate kisses in a baggie in your pocket. While you're checking on your workers' progress, pop a "pep pill" or a "vigor vitamin" in their mouths as you go.

2. Work with your children. Rotate working alongside your children at their assigned chores. They'll love your company, and you can teach them the fine points of the job at hand.

3. Make it fun! One clever mom I read about hid nickels in hard-to-dust places. Only the extra-industrious duster found them.

Another mom of five says that after assigning chores to each person—parents included—they play LOUD sing-along music throughout the house. She says her children enjoy the time—it's a delight to them to see Mom allowing blaring music and joining in the fun.

4. Speak words of encouragement. Nothing works to cheer helpers onward so well as words of honest appreciation and admiration. Say the words "thank you" and "good job" often.

After the Fact

Though you have probably already said "thank you" and "good work" as you went along, it's nice to show extra appreciation when the jobs are completed.

You might post the job list on the refrigerator and provide fancy stickers to paste over their job item to indicate completion. Or you might have a plate of cookies for a morning break—or perhaps a popsicle on a hot day.

If one of your children has really gone beyond the call of duty or excelled in a special way, a quick "Thank you, I noticed" note can be tucked under the child's pillow or in a drawer with socks and hairbands to be found at some later date.

> **My parents showed me a lot about a gracious God. As a result, viewing God as a loving Parent hasn't been a difficult task. To me he is a God who, like my parents, not only has great expectations but who understands my limitations and readily gives needed encouragement.**
> JEAN SHELDON

Job-Swapping

When I (Annette) was a girl, Mom had the five of us children on a rotating job schedule. So, though I had the dreaded bathroom-cleaning job for a whole week, I could look forward to dusting the living room—a job I enjoyed—the next week. I'm sure Mom's ultimate purpose in the job-swapping routine was to be sure that each of us learned about all the elements of housekeeping.

These were some of the assigned daily cleaning jobs I remember from those summer workdays:

Cleaning the bathrooms—sinks, toilets, tubs

Organizing the playroom—putting games and toys in order in the right buckets on the right shelves

Living room, dining room—putting away stray books, toys, and other items, dusting and vacuuming

Windows and mirrors—cleaning designated windows, mirrors, sliding glass doors, and TV screen

"Fingerprinting"—storming the doorframes and light switches with a bucket of suds and a rag to remove smudgy handprints

Dog duty—this job involves messes in the yards (we won't go into detail here . . .)

As older children, we also helped with the laundry— washing, folding, and putting the stacks of clean things on the family member's bed. Each person put his own things in his drawers. We learned to iron, beginning with flat cloth napkins, Daddy's handkerchiefs, and pillowcases.

I felt good about myself that I could do these tasks, that I helped around the house. I could do something for Mom, who was always busy doing things for me. And Dad was proud of us for helping Mom at home.

There are days even now when I enjoy housekeeping (not every time!)—days when the sun shines through the windows on my bright sink faucets and smooth beds and vacuumed or scrubbed floors, days when my muscles seem glad to "make things right." I first felt those same feelings of accomplishment and of a job well done when I was a little girl on the job-swapping schedule. I'm thankful that I have the skills to keep a comfortable home, and I'm thankful that I can stick to a task to get it done. These skills and attitudes toward work have served me well outside the home and in the workplace as well.

Learning Activities

Kitchen Duty

One way of assigning kitchen duty is to rotate it between children. Freddie's on kitchen duty Monday, Wednesday, and Friday, while Frannie helps out on Tuesday, Thursday, and Saturday.

On those unassigned Sundays, or if you choose to work together each night, you might try including songs or word games while you work. We often sang while doing dishes, or we played Bible "Who Am I?" or "What Am I?" Mom (Joyce) would give us a clue, such as, "I was a beauty queen," and each of us would get a chance to guess. If none of us came up with the answer "Esther" from that first clue, Mom would offer a second, such as "I was raised by my uncle Mordecai." Each of us would get another opportunity to guess. And the game would go on until someone guessed. As older children, we knew enough Bible stories and trivia to take turns being the clue-giver.

This game fosters Bible-learning in an enjoyable way and passes the dish-washing and drying time quickly. Challenges on multiplication tables, spelling bees, and other mental activities enhance skills and promote reasoning.

If you choose to work on kitchen clean-up together each night, don't worry that there are not enough jobs to go around. These are some of the ways we divided the evening-meal kitchen chores in our family:

Clearing the table
Scraping dishes (into disposal, garbage can, dog
   dishes)
Washing dishes
Rinsing dishes
Drying dishes
Putting away clean dishes
Scrubbing the stove top and counters
Sweeping the floor

Mom (Joyce) would take a sort of inventory of these tasks as we finished, making sure each job was done and the kitchen was ready for another day's messes.

"Mom, I'm Bored!"

Mom (Joyce) usually responded to this complaint by handing over the silver polish and a cloth! After a while, we learned to make this complaint only when we were *truly* looking for a project—even a work one.

There are more once-in-a-while jobs that children can do—besides polishing the silver. Here are just a few ideas:

Helping to clean the refrigerator
Sorting and stacking the family magazines
Straightening the children's book shelves
Organizing a messy linen cupboard or kitchen drawer
Cleaning the baseboards
Matching clean socks into pairs
Straightening bedroom dresser drawers

The Great Outdoors

Mom (Joyce) had lots of flowers and some occasional vegetables when we were growing up. Though I (Annette) was always glad that the lawn-mowing job mainly fell to my brothers, I did enjoy helping outdoors. Many times all seven of us would be out in the yard together, while Sugar or Tootsie or Butch (whichever dog we had at the time) romped around leashless while we worked. These were some of the major projects we tackled as a family:

Dandelion removal (Dad paid us a penny for each one we picked)

Plucking old vines off a stucco wall

Removing a giant rubber tree from the backyard (with the help of two uncles and a truck)

Leaf raking and bagging

Removing the small stones from the grass and returning them to the rock driveway

Snow shoveling (we each had our own small red shovel)

Cleaning the basement

Organizing the garage

Washing the car

Obviously, not all of these are summertime jobs. But you know best what major jobs need completing around your home. Don't hesitate to make it a family project. Your children will learn to work by working alongside of you—observing your thoroughness, your ability to stick to a job and finish it, and your satisfaction at getting the job done.

Our friend Margie says doing yard work together is one way of enjoying God's world. Celebrating the goodness of God's creation is another excellent reason to work outdoors.

Family Garage Sale

Margie Johnson encourages a late-summer garage sale as an excellent follow-up to summer cleaning projects.

We know from experience that a garage sale can be *lots* of work—especially for Mom. But earning some spare spending money can be a good incentive to help your children sort and organize and part with some of their accumulated "treasures." A family-organized garage sale also gives your children an opportunity to role-play with the world of buying and selling. A good garage sale involves small-scale organization, administration, marketing, and retailing. Let your children come up with ideas for organizing your salable goods, for how you will draw buyers, for deciding how the earned money will be divided.

Our family will never forget our first garage sale. To include even our smallest brother, Brock, in the enterprise, we set him up at the end of the driveway with paper cups and a pitcher of lemonade. Too busy to supervise his sales techniques or business practices, we were a little surprised to discover that he was keeping his earned cash right in the bottom of the lemonade pitcher and was making change by fishing coins out with his own grubby little fist!

Your garage sale will be unique—as unique as your family members and as unique as your family's particular junk.

Looking Ahead to the Holidays

A Minnesota Mom shares this idea: "We make our own Christmas cards—100 each year. We brainstorm ideas, create the card, and produce it in assembly line with everyone helping." She says all of her children have participated in this family tradition since their preschool years.

This is a job well begun in the summer months, since time is needed and enthusiasm may come and go. A family Christmas card can contribute to family unity by working on group creativity, group decision-making, and working as a group toward a family goal. And the work's reward is being able to present many friends and family members with the finished product.

Helping One Another

Assigning a job to two children to do together is another way of building sibling relationships and learning to share and compromise.

I (Annette) remember Saturday mornings when my sister Dawn and I were sent to our bedroom to clean it—together. Once in a while we argued (O.K.—maybe more than once in a while!); and once in a while I'd end up torturing her with tickling. Many times we passed the time showing each other the treasures unearthed from far under the bed or deep on the closet shelves.

I also remember being assigned to Brock, my younger brother, to help him clean his room. I was a good organizer, and he was a spacey little boy with a short attention span for cleaning. You can learn a lot about a brother by sorting through the little-boy treasures in his "junk drawer."

Older children enjoy demonstrating their knowledge by teaching a younger sibling to set the table or tie his shoes. Children will feel good about their knowledge skills when they have an opportunity to "teach" someone else.

Devotional Suggestions

Learning to Work

■ Devotion #1: Work—God's Good Gift

Read and discuss the following Scripture passages that deal with the subject of work. Take one or two passages each time you gather for devotions, depending on the time span that is workable for you and your children. Emphasize that work was a good gift God gave to people—beginning with Adam.

Important Scripture Passages

Genesis 1:26; 2:19-20	Ecclesiastes 5:19
Genesis 2:2; Exodus 23:12	Colossians 3:23-24
Proverbs 6:6-11	2 Thessalonians 3:10
Proverbs 13:4; 20:4	

Wrapping It Up

The following devotional might be helpful in summarizing your Scripture reading of the past week, especially if your children are preschool and lower elementary-school aged.

Johanna—A Real Girl

A long time ago there lived a lovely little girl with great, gray eyes and thick dark-brown braids that hung to her waist. Her name was Johanna, and she lived far across the ocean in the country of Germany with her mother and father and brothers.

Like most of the families that lived in their town, Johanna's family worked very hard. Johanna and her brothers did many jobs both inside and outside their home. Their mother worked long hours cleaning and cooking for the family. She taught Johanna how to clean and cook so she could keep a house when she grew up. Johanna's dad worked hard, too, but he couldn't earn enough money to buy all the food his family needed. Each day the family would eat coarse, black bread with lard (the fat of a pig) and a few vegetables. But each day Johanna would feel hungry.

One day Johanna and her little brother walked far out into the country to do an errand for Father. But on the way home, they took the wrong road. Soon they were lost. They walked and walked. Finally they came to a farmhouse. They knocked on the door to ask the way home. The farmer's wife was very kind and gave each of the children a piece of white bread with butter. Nothing had ever, ever tasted so delicious! *Wouldn't it be wonderful,* wished Johanna, *if we could have white bread every day?*

Then Johanna's father got an important idea. He would take his family far away to the United States of America. "I will work hard there, too," he told Mama. "But maybe I will get paid more money so I can feed my wife and children." Mama agreed.

So Johanna climbed onto a big boat with her whole family and sailed across the water to America.

Many things seemed new to Johanna in America, but many things stayed the same. Johanna's mother still cooked and cleaned and taught Johanna at home. Johanna and her brothers still did many jobs for their family. Father took a job working deep under the ground digging out coal. Every day he worked very hard in the coal mine, and each week he got paid enough money to feed his family. So Johanna ate white bread as well as black—just like she had wished!

Questions to answer and talk about:
In Johanna's family, what was the mother's job?
What kinds of jobs do you think the children did?
Whose job was it to get money to pay for the food for the family?
How did Johanna's parents show they loved their family?
Who do you think helped Johanna's dad get his new job?

———

This devotional might be helpful in summarizing your Scripture reading of the past week if your children are older elementary or junior high aged.

Lazybones

Joey yawned, stretched, and rolled away from the alarm clock's accusing face: 7:35, Friday morning. He'd planned to get up to clean his room before school—he was not allowed out of the house this weekend unless the room was clean, and he had big Friday-night plans with friends. Oh well, he could do it before dinner.

By the time Joey crawled out from under the covers, he had ten minutes to catch his ride to school. So instead of going down to the laundry room to look for the pile of clean clothes his mother had for him, he just grabbed the jeans he'd worn the day before and a rumpled shirt from the back of his desk chair. Oh well, he could dress up next week.

There was no time for the breakfast that waited on the kitchen table. Joey paid 50 cents for a candy bar from the machine at school, remembering how his wrestling coach was encouraging him to lose a few pounds and really get in shape. No time for that today!

Five minutes into first period, he realized that he hadn't even started his history homework for the next hour. So, missing the lecture his Spanish teacher was giving, he quickly scribbled some short answers to the essay questions that had been assigned. Oh well, he'd just spend some extra time reading his Spanish book over the weekend.

After school, he skipped the Student Council meeting he was supposed to attend because he had to get home to clean up his bedroom before dinner. By suppertime, his room was presentable (if Mom didn't inspect it too closely!).

Hold Everything!
What's wrong with Joey's lifestyle?

Getting organized, being involved, and even getting out of bed in the morning take hard work, even discipline. It might sound like something your parents would say, but it's true that God wants his people to be self-controlled and hard-working.

It Won't Kill You!
Here are some hard words of advice for the lazy person:

> *Go to the ant, you sluggard; consider its ways and be wise! It has no commander, no overseer or ruler, yet it stores its provisions in summer and gathers its food at harvest. How long will you lie there, you sluggard? When will you get up from your sleep? A little sleep, a little slumber, a little folding of the hands to rest—and poverty will come on you like a bandit and scarcity like an armed man. Proverbs 6:6-11*

What are some things you discipline yourself to do each day? Why do you make yourself work hard?

God wants you to work hard for his glory. Think about how you can do that today.

> *Whatever you do, work at it with all your heart, as working for the Lord, not for men, since you know that you will receive an inheritance from the Lord as a reward. It is the Lord Christ you are serving. Colossians 3:23-24.**

■ Devotion #2: Responsible to God

Read the story of the three servants and discuss the responsibility to use our energies and talents wisely for the Lord. Search the Scriptures for other references about working in a way that honors God.

Important Scripture Passages
Matthew 25:14-30
Matthew 16:27
1 Corinthians 9:24-25
1 Peter 5:4

Wrapping It Up
The following devotional might be helpful in summarizing your Scripture reading of the past week, especially if your children are preschool and lower elementary-school aged.

Johanna Knows How

When Johanna grew tall and wise, she married handsome Henry. She and Henry lived together in a tiny house not far from town.

"I know how to work hard in the coal mines," Henry said. So he did. He earned money so that he and Johanna could eat.

*Adapted from Annette Heinrich, One in a Zillion, *Shaw, 1990.*

"I know how to make curtains," said Johanna. So she did, and soon their house looked cheerful and charming.

"I know that a clean house is a healthy house," said Johanna. Every day she scrubbed the floors of her little house.

"I know how to take care of chickens," said Johanna and Henry together. So they did. On special days Johanna would fry a chicken for her Henry that was *so* crisp and *so* juicy that even far-away folks heard how wonderful her chicken was!

God sent Henry and Johanna lots and lots of children. "I can love my babies," Johanna said. And she did. Even when she was too busy to carry them, she would wrap them up tight in a warm blanket so they would feel as if Mama's own arms held them.

Now Johanna and Henry worked harder than ever. Johanna got up in the morning dark and went to bed in the dark of night. She would wash her face and fix her hair in the morning dark and was so busy until the night dark that she did not see her own face in a mirror for seven years!

"I know how to bake bread," Johanna said. And so she did. She baked for her own boys and girls, and she baked for her neighbors. Her little boy Billy and his brother Joe would pull Johanna's bread to the other houses in their wagon so they could earn more money for food and clothes.

"I am good in math," said Johanna. "I can start a grocery store." So she did—right in her living room! Handsome Henry built shelves for the cans of food, and people came from all around to shop at Johanna's store.

Johanna and Henry hugged each other tight. "Thank you, God," they prayed, "for helping us know so many things! Thank you that we know how to get food and clothes for our children. Amen."

Questions to answer and talk about:
What things could Henry do?
What things could Johanna do?
Why did they work so hard?
Did Henry and Johanna please God? Why or why not?

———

This devotional might be helpful in summarizing your Scripture reading of the past week if your children are older elementary or junior high aged.

Keeping House

Jana and Lance had made it! For the first time in the history of their sixteen and seventeen years, their parents had left them alone for four days and three nights. Dad had to fly to Hawaii for a sales conference and he'd talked Mom into going along—sort of a second honeymoon. Lance and Jana had urged their mom to go, too—they thought it would be a blast to have the house to themselves.

And it *was* pretty fun—despite Jana's bloopers cooking dinner, Lance locking them both out of the house, and squabbles over who had to change the cat litter (Mom always did it) and who got to drive (Dad always did it).

The day their parents were due back they'd pitched in together to get the house cleaned up (Okay, they'd let things slide just a little . . .). They sorted the stacks of mail, did three loads of laundry, vacuumed the living room, scrubbed the bathroom, and attacked the pile of dirty dishes in the kitchen.

Everything was ready by the time their parents arrived. Jana and Lance acted as if it were nothing when Mom went on and on about the clean house and Dad congratulated them for their "responsibility." Best of all,

Mom and Dad had brought them each a reward: a surfing poster and Waikiki T-shirt for Lance, and tiny opal earrings for Jana.

Good Job, Guys!

In Matthew 25 Jesus tells a story about a man who went on a trip, leaving his three servants in charge. Two of them did a good job with the responsibilities the master had given them, and this is what the boss said when he came home: "Well done, good and faithful servant! You have been faithful with a few things; I will put you in charge of many things. Come and share your master's happiness!" (Matthew 25:21, 23). But one servant wasted his time and his master's money because he was lazy and cowardly. His boss said, "Throw that worthless servant outside, into the darkness, where there will be weeping and gnashing of teeth" (Matthew 25:30).

It's kind of a brutal picture, isn't it? Have you ever been in a situation where you were given a great deal of responsibility? How did you handle it?

According to What You Have Done

Over and over the Bible teaches that God rewards people according to what they have done.

> *For the Son of Man is going to come in his Father's glory with his angels, and then he will reward each person according to what he has done. Matthew 16:27*

> *Without faith it is impossible to please God, because anyone who comes to him must believe that he exists and that he rewards those who earnestly seek him. Hebrews 11:6*

And when the Chief Shepherd appears, you will receive the crown of glory that will never fade away. 1 Peter 5:4

Remember who your Master is and what you're working for. Thank God in advance for the crown of glory that is waiting for you.*

■ Devotion #3: Who's the Boss?
The following Scriptures will spark discussion in the family about working under authority and about recognizing that the ultimate authority is the Lord's.

Important Scripture Passages
Ephesians 6:5-8
Colossians 3:22
1 Timothy 6:1
Titus 2:9-10
1 Peter 2:18-21

Wrapping It Up
The following devotional might be helpful in summarizing your Scripture reading of the past week, especially if your children are preschool and elementary-school aged.

Johanna's Boss

A hard, hard time came to America, even to the place where Johanna and handsome Henry lived. There were not enough jobs for everyone to work. There was not enough food for everyone to eat. There was not enough money to buy clothes and tools.

Adapted from Annette Heinrich, Not a Hollywood Family, Shaw, 1989.

Many people came to Johanna's store. "Johanna," they would say, "our pockets are empty with no money in them. Our stomachs are empty, too. Our feet are tired because we have walked and walked trying to find jobs. But we cannot find any work for pay! You have food in your store, Johanna. Can you help us?"

Johanna began to think, *If I give away my food, my own boys and girls will be hungry and cry. If I give away my money, there will be no warm clothes for my children in the winter.*

But the people needed food—and Johanna had food. And Johanna's heart was full of love. Johanna knew what God taught in his Bible. God says, "If your neighbor comes to borrow from you, and you have something to give him, don't send him away without giving it to him" (Matthew 5:42, paraphrased).

Johanna thought and prayed. "God is the boss," she said. "I will do what he says. He has promised to take care of us. He will help us."

So Johanna obeyed her boss. She shared her food and money with her neighbors. And do you know what? Every one of Johanna's boys and every one of Johanna's girls grew up to be big and strong because they *did* have enough food and they *did* have warm clothes!

Questions to answer and talk about:

A hard time came to America. What did the people need?

Who was Johanna's boss?

Did Johanna obey her boss?

Did God keep his promise to take care of Johanna and Henry's family?

Who is your Boss?

This devotional might be helpful in summarizing your Scripture reading of the past week if your children are older elementary or junior high aged.

Who's the Boss?

Coming in from the fresh outdoors, Pete held his nose as he entered the domain forbidden to all other members of his family: his bedroom. He read the note his mom had scotch-taped to the doorknob: "Peter—whatever it is that has died in there, get it out now! And clean up that room while you're at it."

In his search for the dead "whatever," Pete unearthed three entire loads of dirty laundry, a plastic Coke cup from 7-11 with green fuzz growing deep down at the bottom, and a Christmas mug from last winter complete with hot chocolate streaks.

He figured those items accounted for the smell, so he finished "cleaning" his room by stuffing everything else— ticket stubs, old batteries, school papers, stray socks, crumpled posters, a shoe with no match, worn-down erasers, souvenirs from his class trip to the state capitol, and items he wasn't even sure belonged to him—into his drawers, under the bed, and behind the closet doors.

Just to make a good show of it, he asked Mom for the vacuum cleaner and a dust rag. A quick sweep around the room and he was on his way out the back door!

Not So Fast, Young Man
Pete's mom was not as gullible as he thought. In no time, he was back in his room surveying his pulled-out drawers, open closet door, and a pile dragged from under the bed.

"And this time," said his mom, "I'm going to stay so I'm sure you'll do the job right."

Doing the Job Right

It's important for Peter to learn that even when his mom or a teacher or boss isn't looking, God is. And God expects him to do good work—for the Lord's sake.

Slaves, obey your earthly masters with respect and fear, and with sincerity of heart, just as you would obey Christ. Obey them not only to win their favor when their eye is on you, but like slaves of Christ, doing the will of God from your heart. Serve wholeheartedly, as if you were serving the Lord, not men, because you know that the Lord will reward everyone for whatever good he does, whether he is slave or free. Ephesians 6:5-8

Have you ever done a good job—even when no one was around to pat you on the back? The Scriptures also say that doing a good job is a good testimony—that others will react positively to your story of Christ just because you are a diligent worker.

Teach slaves to be subject to their masters in everything, to try to please them, not to talk back to them, and not to steal from them, but to show that they can be fully trusted, so that in every way they will make the teaching about God our Savior attractive. Titus 2:9-10

Hang in there as you work this week. Ask God to make you patient and thorough to get the job done right.

Loving Jesus by Serving Others
Section 3

Serving Together

If only generosity came as easily as selfishness does! Each of us will battle selfishness at different times in our lives, and it will benefit your children to begin early to learn some lessons of self*less*ness.

At first, it may seem like a strange idea to *plan* thoughtfulness onto a calendar, but our family did just that. We marked a day far enough ahead of Grandma's birthday to make sure her cards and gifts were mailed on time. We set aside part of an afternoon to shop for Dad's birthday presents and to wrap them. We designated Wednesdays from 10:30-11:30 A.M. for letter writing, to ensure that we wrote thank-you notes and sent birthday and anniversary greetings. And the children would write notes or draw pictures in order to keep in touch with a far-away family member.

Planning thoughtfulness makes it happen. And planning thoughtfulness gets children involved. Hopefully your kids will absorb the concept that thinking about and serving others is a task that we address as a normal part of our Christian life.

And speaking of serving others, service and ministry must also be planned into summer days. Our family's trips to a senior citizen's complex, Vacation Bible School, and a Five-Day Club all provided opportunities for the children to serve and were sources of spiritual growth for them as well.

One of my most urgent prayers to the Lord over the years has been: "Lord, glorify yourself in our children. Glorify yourself in this family." Even now as they begin families of their own, the heart cry has not changed; it has only expanded to include the new members. "Glorify yourself, Lord, in our family—and in their families!"

My heart echoes the song based on David's heart desire: "One thing have I desired of the Lord." The one thing I have desired is that my children may love and serve Jesus and glorify him all the days of their lives.

The activities and devotions in this section will do just that—bring glory to God through your family not only *now*, but by his help and grace, will build understandings and set attitudes that will enable your children to glorify Jesus all the days of their lives.

> **Learning to care for others
> is a spiritual discipline that requires
> nurturing. Our responsibility as
> parents is to help our children become
> tender toward the less fortunate,
> especially those who still don't know
> Christ as their Savior.**
> PAT PALAU

Learning Activities

Teaching about Giving

When I (Annette) was about five years old, Mom bought a wonderful doll that came in a compact, blue carrying case complete with a change of doll clothes. I sat on her bed and watched her wrap it up to send to another little girl—a Korean child whom our family sponsored.

"But I want that doll, Mom!" I confessed glumly, eyeing that blue carrying case with envy.

"That's what makes it a good gift, Annie," she explained. "God doesn't want us to give old leftover junk when we serve him. He wants us to give good things— our best, things we would like ourselves. When we give our best work for him, it makes God happy."

That package was mailed, and I felt only the slightest twinge of jealousy. I understood enough to feel glad that we were serving the Lord. Later I learned that the other little girl had not even been permitted to keep that wonderful doll; it had become a toy for all the children at the orphanage to share.

That was a good early lesson for me in giving and in thinking about what it would be like to be someone else—someone without toys, someone without her own home. No doubt that earlier lesson served to prepare me to tackle bigger lessons in understanding and giving, when that Korean girl became my own sister.

What a blessing God gave us in sending us Dawn, our sister and friend! Our small gifts for God never do come close to his good and perfect gifts to us.

> **Plant seeds of spiritual truth
> so that they grow in your child's fertile
> mind—and bear good fruit.**
> RITA SCHWEITZ

Serving Others at Home

It's important to cultivate a sense of serving one another at home. The place where you live is the place where you will have the most opportunities to serve the Lord by serving others. Praise your children for their acts of kindness or helpfulness. Help them to realize that their service pleases God.

We Heinrich children could tell stories about some of the unique methods Mom (Joyce) employed to teach us to be kind to one another. Some were rather dismal failures and were quickly given up. Others really did work, though, and were some of our more memorable lessons in serving one another.

Once when we were very young, Mom placed a small gold carriage on the kitchen table and a bowl of bright beads beside it. She explained that each time one of us did something nice for someone else in the family without telling anybody—not even her—then we could come quietly to the kitchen and put a "jewel" in the carriage. The goal was to fill the carriage with serving deeds by a certain date (you could set aside any one of the summer months for a similar project).

It didn't take us long to catch Mom's enthusiasm for the project. For a few weeks the five of us sneaked about the house, serving one another. I sorted and arranged my sisters' shoes in their closet. I went upstairs to make my bed and found it neatly done, complete with my best doll propped against the pillow. Somebody cleaned the bathroom when it wasn't his turn.

I'll admit that when the carriage was filled and the project completed, we didn't keep rushing around to do good deeds for one another. But we had learned the pleasure of sharing small kindnesses—kindnesses that only the Lord could know about. And we had experienced the good feelings that come with doing something for others.

Go Ahead, Make Someone's Day!

It's important to teach your children to think about other's lives and other's needs. Most children have imaginations strong enough to help them "walk in somebody else's shoes" for a few minutes.

When I (Annette) wanted to keep that doll for myself instead of sending such a nice toy off to an orphanage, Mama asked me, "Would you want to receive a present that was a used and dirty doll?" Of course I didn't! I could imagine how I'd feel if someone gave me a used-up present.

Your children can help you brainstorm about how to help another person or another family. Maybe your school-aged son will think of taking another child of the same age to the movies or the science museum—because those are things he likes to do. Maybe your preschooler will suggest buying a sticker book for a sick friend—because that's what she would want if she had to spend a day in bed.

It's also important to model creative caring. Your children will take notice and observe the way that you serve others. For example, I (Annette) can remember Mom sending a plate of Christmas cookies over to the neighbors—neighbors who had robbed our house while we were on vacation the summer before! I've seen her prepare extra Easter baskets with goodies and tiny gifts for three little girls down the street, whose father had a long-term illness and whose mother was worn out with caring for him and the girls. These were given anonymously, from "A Secret Friend." That mystery was a delight to those little girls!

Provide your children with opportunities to practice creative caring. Help your children develop expertise in serving others for Jesus' sake.

Helping a Sick Friend

One family showed their love and support for a family friend confined to a wheelchair. Mom and the kids brainstormed together about what they could do to help. They went as a team to clean her house, cook meals, watch her children, or take them places she could not take them, like the park or the zoo.

This kind of teamwork strengthens family unity at the same time that it cultivates creativity in service.

Bringing Gladness to a Nursing Home

It's important to provide your children with opportunities to think about others' lives and to experience relationships with people who are different from themselves, including people who are older or younger than they are.

I (Annette) remember the first time Mom took us to a convalescent hospital, where we visited the very elderly mother of our pastor. Frankly, I was scared. There were people there who didn't act, well, *normal*. There were people who stared—at me or at nothing at all. There were people who made spoken noises that weren't real "talking." There were people whose clothes seemed messy and dull, and some who didn't look or smell very nice.

Mom explained that there are some things we do for other people and not for ourselves. She helped us to imagine ourselves in old Mrs. Churchill's situation. She couldn't ever go outside anymore. She couldn't remember events or people very well. There was little to make one day different from another for Mrs. Churchill. Suddenly our young lives took on a great deal of color and variety in our estimation. We saw that we had something we didn't even know we had—lots of options. And we saw that maybe we did have something valid to offer to Grandma Churchill.

I don't remember what we took to Grandma Churchill, but I remember other times when we made tissue-paper flower bouquets and took them to older neighbors. Mom regularly planned a field trip for her first graders to take flower baskets with hard candies and love notes tucked inside to nursing home residents.

Paper flowers last a long time. Practice a song, make a poster, bake cookies, learn a Bible verse to recite—all these are welcome contributions to help light up a life. Perhaps a person whose physical limitations keep him or her confined to bed or to a small cubicle would benefit from your children's creativity and generosity. And perhaps your children will benefit from "stepping in their shoes" for a few moments.

Oops!

Do you ever worry that your efforts at serving someone else will go wrong? Perhaps the friend will feel criticized or offended if you offer to mow his lawn. Perhaps you'll overcook the roast beef dinner you've promised to cook for an elderly shut-in. Perhaps a friend will feel obligated to you for your service, even though you meant it as a love-gift with no strings attached. Lots of things can go haywire when you stick your neck out for love.

But don't let worries about mistakes discourage you from obeying God's command to serve others. Our family has a long history of boo-boos that turned out O.K. in the end.

Mom (Joyce) has a habit of escaping to the bathtub in the late evenings. In the tub she reads and worships. It doesn't surprise us to hear a soft worship song come floating out over the bubbles and splashes in there. One Tuesday night, Mom was startled in the middle of her tub-time reading by an idea that she felt was a clear instruction from the Lord. One little girl in her public school first-grade class—we'll call her Cindy—had shared with Mom regularly about her daddy's search for a job. Mom knew that Cindy was a Christian, and she prayed with her for a job for her daddy. That night in the tub, Mom felt a strong desire to provide some groceries for Cindy's family.

Of course Dad agreed with the plan. The five of us kids, then in junior high and high school, groaned at being dragged along. But it was Wednesday evening, and the stop was on the way to our mid-week youth group Bible study.

Mom got the child's address, and Dad drove us to Cindy's neighborhood—literally on the other side of the tracks in our town. In the dusk it was difficult for us to make out the numbers on the houses, so we were glad when Mom spotted the little girl sitting on the steps of a house about where her house should be.

Mom didn't want Cindy to know that her teacher was bringing the gift; it wouldn't do to have the story spread to the other children in their class at school. So Mom scrunched down on the floor of the car, and the rest of us got out and started unloading the bags of groceries.

The man on the porch spoke limited English, and Dad had a hard time convincing him that the groceries were really a gift. "For me? For me?" he kept repeating.

Cindy herself ran to the car and—ironically—directly to the passenger seat door, which she opened. She was delighted to see her teacher (though the teacher wasn't so delighted at being caught in that undignified position!).

"Oh, Mrs. Heinrich! Won't you come to visit my family? We live over there!" Cindy exclaimed, pointing to the house next door.

We were delivering groceries to the wrong house! Dad was red-faced as he explained the mistake to the man on the porch. Fortunately, all the neighbors realized that Cindy's father was out of work and in need of the food. He gladly helped us move the bags.

Now that she was found out, Mom greeted Cindy's mother, who cried and told us, "Last night I prayed and asked God to show us he still cared about us. It has been so long since my husband worked. I thought God didn't care anymore. Now I know that he loves us and cares about us!"

So, despite our clumsiness with the whole effort, Mom's obedience to God's command was important for that family. In fact, it was a direct answer to their prayer. And it was certainly a memorable—even if laughable—lesson in giving for all of us. Don't let awkwardness or embarrassment keep you from doing your best to serve the Lord and becoming an answer to someone's prayers.

Earned Treasure

Even if you don't have lots of money to provide groceries or some other necessity for a needy person, there are acts of service that you and your children can provide. Who knows better than you do how much energy your children have? That childhood sturdiness and energy can come in handy for those who no longer can do physical labor for themselves.

A friend from Minnesota told us that their whole family—mom, dad, and two children—chopped and stacked a huge pile of wood for their grandpa, who called the work a "treasure hunt." When the job was finished and four tired people sat down to rest, Grandpa explained that the treasure at the end of the hunt was "a job well done." They agreed and also shared the treasure of good feelings about being able to help their grandfather.

Your children have so much to offer! In this case, the children were generous with their time and energy in order to serve their grandfather. The younger people could supply something they had that their grandpa needed—strength to tackle a big job. Grandpa's warm winter evenings beside his fire will remind him of the blessing of his grandchildren's loving service.

Another family we know "adopted" an elderly woman from their church, taking on her outdoor work and many of the housekeeping chores as well. This mom was overjoyed to overhear one son comment to the other that helping "Grandma" was fun.

Giving Yourself

When you don't have a lot of money to give, you can think creatively about what you *do* have to share.

I (Joyce) left a classroom of beloved children in Fresno, California when we moved to another town. They were young; most were sons and daughters of parents who had immigrated to the United States two or three years earlier. The children came to me with sadness to say good-bye, expressing how much they wished they could buy something for me. I knew that feeling. I empathized with their desire to give more than they could. They were young children. What *could* they give? I expected nothing.

But they did give! One brought wildflowers; one brought a chain made from rubberbands. Some drew pictures. One brought me a quarter. Some showed me how much they had learned by writing letters. And many of the girls brought small pieces of needlework they had stitched themselves.

I was overwhelmed to receive such love gifts. Because the gifts were products of their creative abilities and time spent, they meant more to me than all the fine china or perfume that money would have purchased.

When you give yourself, you have given the ultimate gift.

Open Home

We Heinrich children learned so much about the world from the people who brought other nations and cultures right to our doorstep. We often had visiting missionaries stay with us—so often in fact that sometimes Mom would forget to tell us kids when someone was coming. I remember coming home late one evening to discover an unfamiliar man's shaving kit in the bathroom. I tiptoed to my own room and peeked in—just to make sure that whoever it was wasn't sleeping in my bed!

Friends of ours in Illinois opened their home to a family newly arrived from Vietnam. She says that whenever her three-bedroom house seems too crowded for her family with five children, she remembers how that family of five asked to live in the 8 x 10 storage shed in her back yard. And she's thankful for an added plus—that her children found common interests with these children from another culture and background.

Do people feel welcome in your home? Brainstorm with your children about ways you could make your home a place where people will come to share.

Serving the Lord at Church

There are many ways you and your family can serve at church. Some things you can do together as a family, but be sure to encourage your children to serve in their own areas of interest.

One family we know takes a turn cleaning their church every other month. It's a heavy-duty job, but they work together to get it done.

Your family might undertake a project such as painting a Sunday school classroom, or sorting and organizing a storage area.

Some moms and dads share nursery duty with their older children. This can be a great opportunity for your son or daughter to learn about infant or childcare in a well-supervised environment.

My brother Marc was an usher when he was twelve or thirteen. I (Annette) worked with preschoolers in the nursery by the time I was eleven. Older children and teens can be a great help with younger children during special missions conferences or Vacation Bible School. As junior highers, my brother and sister Brock and Adele both worked with younger children in a summer program. I taught my first Sunday school class when I was in the ninth grade.

Encourage your children to take part in church workdays or youth group work projects. Many churches have programs that assign a young person to do projects for an elderly church member or an invalid.

Of course, the best way to encourage your children to serve in God's house is to be involved yourself. Ask your church leaders about service projects available to your family.

Give and Get with a Five-Day Club

There was *so* much to do to get ready for our Five-Day Club—an at-home, neighborhood evangelism Bible school. The children had seen Bob and me (Joyce) involved in evangelism training and outreach ministry, and now it was their turn. Here was a ministry to help them tell *their* friends about Jesus.

The children and I filled out the invitations together. They hand-delivered them house to house, saying personally, "Hope you can come." They helped me bake cookies, mix pitchers of Kool-Aid, and set up the patio outside with chairs and an easel.

When the boys and girls started coming at the set time, our family acted as hosts and hostesses, greeting and staying with others until the leader took charge of the club time.

There were many opportunities for the children to give in putting on a Five-Day Club. Yet look how much they received:

Some friends received Jesus as Savior.
All the children learned Bible truths and Bible verses.
Some children received awards and prizes for attendance and memorization.
All had fun singing peppy songs, hearing suspenseful stories, eating yummy snacks, and just being together.
My children had the joy of serving and witnessing.

Check your local directory for the phone number and address of the Child Evangelism Fellowship in your area. It is likely that they can provide Five-Day Club service to your home by sending a teacher complete with stories and games and prizes. If not, you might consider getting together with another ambitious mom to combine the roles of teacher, Bible-memory coach, hostess, etc.

The Poor and Needy

Friends of ours who live in Wheaton have an annual Thanksgiving tradition in their family. Mom, dad, and the three sons all spend the night together at a shelter for the homeless, where they help serve the free Thanksgiving meal to people who have no turkey, stuffing, and cranberries—and not even a kitchen table of their own to eat at. Those children experience real thankfulness for their lovely home near the forest, for their warm beds, and for the bounty of food that is always at hand.

Most of today's older children will be well aware that there are homeless people and people who go hungry—right here in the United States. As a family devotions project, you might research the vast number of Scripture references that command God's people to care for the poor and needy.

Another concrete way to show commitment to the needy is to sponsor a child. At any given time over the years our family sponsored one or two needy children in another country by sending a monthly check and an occasional gift or letter. There were times when we planned, as a family, ways of coming up with that monthly money. For a while all seven of us gave up Saturday lunch. Mom took the sting out of this by serving a late breakfast and an early supper, but it was a lesson in sympathy for us to feel hungry for an hour or two in the meantime.

Small Kindnesses

Isaiah 32:2 says that "Each man will be like a shelter from the wind and a refuge from the storm, like streams of water in the desert and a shadow of a great rock in a thirsty land." The world we live in is certainly a land thirsting for God's love and for the refreshing streams of the ministry of his people.

Help your children remember that even the most everyday activities are part of serving the Lord. You will model this serving mentality by practicing kindness—a sympathetic word to the young man who is pumping your gas during a thunderstorm, cheerful patience in the face of a rude salesclerk, a cold Coca-cola for the woman mowing the apartment lawn, a brownie for the tired UPS delivery man. (See Proverbs 12:25.) As often as possible, let your children be a part of that kindness. Let your child deliver the cold drink or help prepare and deliver a dinner for a sick friend.

Each of us knows how a loving action can soothe when a day has been filled with disappointments or anxiety. Learning to serve in our everyday actions is part of "doing unto others."

Learning to Receive

While your children are learning about giving to and serving others, it is important that they learn to understand how the receivers of their service might feel. When your family receives kindnesses from others, make a point of calling attention to the way God has blessed your family through his people.

Our family has received more than our share, we think! We have seen God's goodness to us through his servants consistently over the years. And we delight at being held so closely in his care.

It seemed as if the very arms of Jesus himself slipped around us as we opened a check from the church during a long period of unemployment. What a tremendous ministry it was to have church young people help load our moving van on one end of a move and then be met by the young people of our new church to help unload at the other end! This is God's love in action and one of the many joys of being a member of God's dear family. As we remember back over the years, the list of kindnesses grows longer and longer.

When new babies arrived, so did church friends with meals and gifts and loving words about the baby. Some even took time to do housekeeping chores.

When desperate, painful experiences came to our family, the church was a stalwart support with prayers and calls and encouragement—and sometimes plants and flowers and cards.

Each loving act says loud and clear, "I love you. God loves you. I care. He cares."

Commenting aloud to the children about these kindnesses—thanking God during grace or devotions for each thoughtful friend, for each gift to meet your need—makes a powerful statement to them about the effects and importance of serving Jesus and the kind of God who motivates people to live this way.

Devotional Suggestions

Serving Others

■ Devotion #1: God Knows

Help your children to understand that when you as a family or they as individuals serve the Lord, it's not for personal glory or a pat on the back. Help them to understand that we serve to make God happy, to show that we love him, and to help others know him. Remind them that even when no one else is looking, God knows that they are serving him. The following Scriptures are instructive passages or Bible stories that illustrate that we serve God and not people.

Important Scripture Passages
Jeremiah 17:10
Matthew 6:1-4
Luke 21:1-4
1 Timothy 3:13
1 Timothy 6:17-19
Hebrews 6:10-11
Revelation 2:19, 23

Wrapping It Up
The following devotional might be helpful in summarizing your Scripture reading of the past week, especially if your children are preschool and lower elementary-school aged.

A Kiss on the Cheek

"Mama!" called Missy from the doorway. "Where are you?"

"In the kitchen, Missy. I'm getting ready to make brownies for Aunt Marilyn. She's bringing the baby over for a visit. Would you like to help?"

Missy dashed off to wash her hands. It was fun to bake with Mama; it was even more fun to have the baby come for a visit!

While Missy and Mama mixed the sugar and butter and cracked the eggs, they talked.

"Sometimes, Mama," said Missy, "I just wish Jesus could come for a visit like Aunt Marilyn. I wish he could just come in our door so I could hug him and give him a kiss on the cheek. I love him so much!"

Mama turned off the mixer and hugged Missy. "Why, Missy. You feel exactly the way I feel. I wish Jesus could come visit, too. In fact, I have a secret of what I do when I am wishing I could give him a hug or a kiss on the cheek."

Mama sat down and snuggled Missy on her lap. Mama showed Missy a verse from her Bible. "Jesus is talking in this part of the Bible, Missy. He says, 'If you do something kind to someone, it is just like you did it for me!' " (Matthew 25:40, paraphrased).

Then Mama whispered in Missy's ear, "This is my secret, Missy. My secret is that I find someone to do a kind deed for—a little, quiet kindness. After I do it, I don't tell anyone, but I just say to God, " 'That was a kiss on your cheek!' "

The doorbell rang, and Missy dashed off again, this time to welcome Aunt Marilyn and baby David.

After lunch and brownies and a visit together, Missy lay down to rest. Baby David was in the next room fussing and crying a little. Because Mama and

Aunt Marilyn were washing the dishes, they didn't hear him.

Missy slipped quietly up to his cradle. She pushed it gently and sang, "Rock-a-bye David, on the treetop." As she sang and the cradle rocked, David shut his tired eyes and fell fast asleep. Missy pulled the blanket up to his fat little chin and tiptoed away, saying, "That was a kiss on the cheek, Jesus!"

Questions to answer and talk about:
Who was coming to visit Missy and Mama?
Who did Missy say she wished could come for a visit?
What did she want to give to Jesus? Why?
What did Jesus say in Mama's Bible verse?
What was Mama's secret?
What kind deed did Missy do?
Do you think she told Mama or Aunt Marilyn about it?
How can we show our love for Jesus?

———

This devotional might be helpful in summarizing your Scripture reading of the past week if your children are older elementary or junior high aged.

Just a Jock

Bart's dad was an ex-All-American athlete and a high school athletics coach, so Bart had learned to say, "Batter up!" and "Touchdown" almost before he said "Mama!" He played little league baseball and soccer, and by the time he was in junior high, he was playing football, too. By high school he was playing football in the fall and baseball in the spring, and was wrestling in between. When he wasn't at a team practice, he was home shooting hoops in the driveway or playing tennis at the sports club with his brother.

Athletics were Bart's first love, and schoolwork wasn't a close second. Studying didn't come easy for him, but he brought home C's and B's and managed to stay eligible for all the extra-curricular sports activities he wanted to participate in.

So most of his friends at school and most of his relatives, too, classified him in their minds and conversations as a jock—just a "jock."

Clark Kent

But Bart has more to him than meets the eye. Like the quiet, unassuming newspaperman Clark Kent, who ducks into a phone booth and becomes Superman, Bart quietly commits his days and weeks to serving God.

The first time Bart went to the children's ward at the hospital he visited his favorite little cousin, Amelia, who was ill for a long time. His creative weekly visits became more frequent, and Amelia and all the other kids loved his crazy antics and unexpected games and activities. He'd arrive loaded with picture books, balloons, puzzles, and even homemade videos of the great outdoors and of the kids themselves. When Amelia went home, the doctors and nurses told Bart they would be sorry to see him go. But by then Bart was hooked, and he kept on visiting.

Secret SuperServant

Do you ever feel labeled by teachers or students at school? By your family members? How do they see you? Are their labels for you on target, or is there more to you than meets the eye?

> *"Be careful not to do your 'acts of righteousness' before men, to be seen by them. If you do, you will have no reward from your Father in*

> *heaven. . . . But when you give to the needy, do not let your left hand know what your right hand is doing, so that your giving may be in secret. Then your Father, who sees what is done in secret, will reward you." Matthew 6:1, 3-4*

> *God is not unjust; he will not forget your work and the love you have shown him as you have helped his people and continue to help them. We want each of you to show this same diligence to the very end, in order to make your hope sure. Hebrews 6:10-11*

Don't be discouraged if others don't give you credit for all you really are and for your service to others. Remember that God knows all about your true character and that your hard work is service for him.*

■ Devotion #2: Equipped to Serve

The following Scripture passages and devotion suggestions will help to remind your children that they are not serving the Lord on their own strengths and abilities but that God promises to be with them and to provide his Holy Spirit to strengthen and uphold them.

Important Scripture Passages

Joshua 1:9	Philippians 4:13
Matthew 11:28-30	Colossians 1:10-12
Acts 1:8	1 Peter 4:11
Ephesians 6:10-18	2 Timothy 2:15; 3:14-17

Wrapping It Up

The following devotional might be helpful in summarizing your Scripture reading of the past week, especially

Adapted from Annette Heinrich, One in a Zillion, Shaw, 1990.

if your children are preschool and lower elementary-school aged.

Hidden Treasure

"Sugar is missing! Sugar is missing!" One child passed the word to another until everyone in the family had heard the sad news. Sugar, their beloved, shaggy dog was gone, and no one could find her. They had called for her all over the neighborhood and down in the woods behind the house. Not one whimper did they hear, nor any happy panting, nor any loud bark. Only quiet answered their calls.

"Dad, what if her pups come while she is gone?" Danny asked, for Sugar was going to have puppies any day.

Sandi was almost afraid to say, "Maybe she is hurt and needs our help!"

All the children began to pray that Sugar would be safe and her baby pups, too.

Even while they were praying, the doorbell rang. Mr. Andrews from next door was there with a big smile on his face. "I think you all might like to know that I have a hidden treasure in my yard," he said. "Come on over, and I will show it to you!"

In their excitement, the children forgot about their sad problem. They slipped on their jackets so they could go see the hidden treasure. What could it be?

Mr. Andrews led them to his enormous evergreen tree. "Look underneath my tree," he said.

As they peeked beneath the long green branches, they gave a giant cheer!

"Sugar!" they all cried. "It's Sugar!" There, deep against the trunk of the evergreen, Sugar had dug a shallow hole and lined it with her own soft, white fur. In this nest she had snuggled four new pups! What a wonderful hidden treasure!

As they carried the new pups home in a blanket-lined basket, Sugar kept "counting" them with her nose to make sure her babies were all there.

"How did Sugar know how to build a nest, Dad?" Danny wanted to know. "How did Sugar think of using her own fur?"

Sandi couldn't understand why Sugar hadn't come when they called her. "She must have heard our voices!"

"Sugar knows how to have pups and take care of them because God gave her the 'I-know-how' right inside of her," explained Dad. "You might say that God has put a hidden treasure inside of her so she would know how to make a nest and so she wouldn't leave her babies alone even when she was called. We call that I-know-how in animals 'instinct.'

"God gave people an even more wonderful kind of hidden treasure than animals get," Dad went on. "When boys and girls ask Jesus to forgive their sins and be their God, he gives them a treasure that he promises never to take away from them. It is the hidden treasure of the Holy Spirit. The Holy Spirit comes right into the heart of us and never, ever goes away again. He gives us help and reminds us of God's rules. He gives us ideas how to help other people, and he gives us courage when we need to be brave."

"Like when I was getting my tonsils out and had to go to the operating room without Mom or Dad," remembered Sandi.

"Right—and when I had to say that long part for the Sunday school program and I felt afraid," said Danny.

The children began to remember times when the Holy Spirit had taught them and helped them.

They prayed together for the second time that day. "Dear Jesus, thank you that Sugar is home safe again, and thank you for her beautiful puppies. Thank you for the hidden treasure you put in her to help her know how to take care of her babies. And thank you most of all for the wonderful hidden treasure in us, the Holy Spirit of God! We sure love you, Jesus. Amen."

Questions to answer and talk about:
What was the hidden treasure under Mr. Andrews's tree?
What was Sugar's hidden treasure inside of her?
What hidden treasure does God give people?
Do all people get this treasure? Who does, and who doesn't?
How does the Holy Spirit help us?

———

This devotional might be helpful in summarizing your Scripture reading of the past week if your children are older elementary or junior high aged.

Be Prepared!

Melissa climbed on the school bus and settled into the nearest seat with her best friend, Liz. She had big plans for her first year of Junior High School—plans to learn a lot and to improve her grades. When they arrived at school, Melissa offered to carry Liz's back-pack, since Liz's hands were full with her lunchsack and a notebook.

In homeroom, the teacher passed out cards for the students to fill out with personal information and class schedules. Melissa was embarrassed to realize that all of the other students had pens and pencils, but she borrowed one from the teacher and didn't worry.

In Language Arts Melissa had to borrow a pencil and paper from a friend. She did the same thing in Spanish 1. Third period she had Physical Education. She was surprised when Liz and her other friends began to change into bright yellow t-shirts and black gym shorts. "Didn't you read the letter they sent you at home?" asked Liz.

At lunch time, Melissa realized that she hadn't brought a lunch or money to buy it at the cafeteria.

By the end of that first day, she was hungry and grumpy—and tired of carrying around loose papers with no notebooks to keep them in.

Get Ready!

Melissa should have thought ahead to the challenges of life in Junior High. When your mom goes to bake a cake, she checks over the recipe to make sure she has the ingredients necessary. When a builder constructs a skyscraper, he makes sure that he's got all the materials it will take to make that building reach for the clouds. A worker needs to be equipped with the tools for the job.

God doesn't expect you to serve him without providing you with the equipment you need to do the job right. God promises to be with you, to give you the necessary strength and creativity through his Spirit. And he's given you the Bible, an instruction manual for those who want to serve the Lord.

> *If anyone serves, he should do it with the strength God provides, so that in all things God may be praised through Jesus Christ.*
> *1 Peter 4:11b*

> *All Scripture is God-breathed and is useful for teaching, rebuking, correcting and training in righteousness, so that the man of God may be thoroughly equipped for every good work.*
> *2 Timothy 3:16-17*

Be Courageous!
When you're nervous about serving God, remember that you are not working alone and in your own power. God is with you, and he promises to help.

> *"Be strong and courageous. Do not be terrified; do not be discouraged, for the LORD your God will be with you wherever you go."*
> *Joshua 1:9b*

■ Devotion #3: Thinking of Others First

The following Scriptures remind God's people to think of others' needs and wants, which is the essential first step to serving others. These passages will encourage you and your family as you practice creative service this summer.

If your children are older, you might want to make a Scripture search for all the "one another" Scriptures in the New Testament. An older child might be placed in charge of keeping the family's list. The vast number of instructions to "love one another," "serve one another," "forgive one another," etc. will encourage your family to be conscious of others.

Important Scripture Passages
Romans 12:9-11
Galatians 5:13-14
Philippians 2:3-11
Luke 10:30-37

Wrapping It Up
The following devotional might be helpful in summarizing your Scripture reading of the past week, especially if your children are preschool and lower elementary-school aged.

Sunshine Boarding School
(A play in two acts based on Philippians 2:3-11)

To put on this play you will need:

Introduction: a dustmop
                     a diploma (roll a sheet of white paper and tie with a ribbon)
                     a book

Act 1:   papers and pencils
                     a little bell

Act 2:   a long sheet of paper
                     a plastic cup
                     another plastic cup with big pieces cut out of it
                     a broom
                     a rag
                     a can of bandages

The actors: The Narrator
                     Dr. M. Portant, Headmaster of the School
                     Miss Prim, the Teacher
                     Mr. Dustmop, the Janitor
                     Boys and Girls

Introduction

(The Narrator, Dr. Portant, Miss Prim, and Mr. Dustmop stand together)

Narrator: Far out in the country by a shady, splashy pool
                     Sat an ivy-covered building, the Sunshine Boarding School.

                     There the laddies and the lassies learned their lessons every day
                     From young Miss Prim, their teacher,

who had quite a lot to say.
(Miss Prim is holding a book. She
bows.)

Dr. Portant, the stern principal, was
tall and very grim.
He was the boss of everyone—yes,
even of Miss Prim!
(Dr. Portant is holding a diploma. He
bows.)

Mr. Dustmop cleaned the building
and kept it shiny bright.
But while he worked, when things
went wrong, he always made them
right!
(Mr. Dustmop is holding a dustmop.
He bows.)

A peek within the red brick walls of
Sunshine Boarding School
Will help us learn what Jesus
taught, the "Love Your Neighbor"
Rule.
(All exit. Set up classroom for Act 1.)

Act 1

Scene 1, The Classroom
(Boys and girls are seated at desks or pretend desks.
They each have pencils and papers. Miss Prim is stand-
ing in front of the class.)

Miss Prim: Now Boys and Girls, I hope you
studied very hard for your
arithmetic test today. If you do a
good job, Dr. Portant will think I

am a good and wonderful teacher.
(Miss Prim fluffs her hair. The boys
and girls do not understand. They
look at each other, shrug, and
scratch their heads.)

Now make me look good! Ready,
begin!
(Boys and girls write on their papers
for a few moments. Miss Prim
rings the little bell.)

Time is up. Bring your papers to me.
You may go.
(The boys and girls go out.)

Scene 2, The Hallway
(Mr. Dustmop is holding his mop. He meets the children
in the hall.)

Mr. Dustmop: Hi, Boys and Girls. Was your test
hard? Do you think you did a good
job? I hope you did! You will all
need to know arithmetic so you
can get good jobs and make good
homes when you grow up!
(Boys and girls smile and nod their
heads. Set up classroom for
Act 2.)

Act 2

(In the classroom, the boys and girls are sitting at their
desks. Miss Prim is at the back of the room. Dr. Portant
is at the front of the class. He is holding a long sheet of
paper.)

Dr. Portant: Boys and girls, today I will be teaching you all the rules for the playground.
(He coughs rather hard and long.)

Would somebody please get me a glass of water?
(A small boy brings a glass of water from the back of the room, but he trips and falls. Then he cries. He has broken the glass and skinned his knee. He sits up and holds the "broken" glass, still crying.)

I am too important to clean up this mess.
(He calls Mr. Dustmop in a loud voice).

Mr. Dustmop! Mr. Dustmop!
Miss Prim, will you *please* help that boy?
(Miss Prim stays in the same place, but shows him the back of her hands.)

Miss Prim: I can't help him. I might break my pretty red fingernails.
(She calls Mr. Dustmop in a loud voice.)

Mr. Dustmop! Mr. Dustmop!
(Mr. Dustmop comes in. He is carrying a rag, a broom, and a can of bandages. He bends down by the hurt boy.)

Mr. Dustmop: I am sorry you are hurt, my friend. Let me put a bandage on that knee.

          (He puts the bandage on, then helps
          the boy to his seat. He begins to
          clean up the mess. He cleans
          while the Narrator reads the
          closing lines.

Narrator: I'm wondering what lessons *we* may
          have learned today?
          Who loved his neighbor? Who did
          not? You be the one to say.
          Let's talk about these questions and
          the "Love Your Neighbor" Rule.
          Which people pleased the Savior at
          the Sunshine Boarding School?

Questions to answer and talk about:

In Act 1, who thought about the interests of others, Miss Prim or Mr. Dustmop?

In Act 2, who thought he was more important than others? Who thought others were more important than himself?

In Act 2, who was selfish? How? Who was unselfish? How?

In the whole play, who was a servant like Jesus? Who would not be a servant?

————

This devotional might be helpful in summarizing your Scripture reading of the past week if your children are older elementary or junior high aged.

Speak Up!

Samantha is pretty, there's no doubt about it. And she is lively and creative. She can make a boring bus trip into "Whacky Wildness on Wheels" or turn a dismal rained-out youth group picnic from a flop into "Fun without Sun!" It's no big surprise that she's popular.

Now if you're thinking, *Gag! I'll bet that Samantha's a stuck-up fathead!* you're wrong. All things considered, she's a nice girl with lots of gifts who loves the Lord. In fact, she knows who to thank for her gift of gab and her ability to enjoy people and activities—God!

Different

One of Samantha's biggest challenges is to remember that not everyone feels right at home in a group, that not everyone feels accepted or that they "fit."

Two months ago, a girl named Emily started coming to youth group activities at Samantha's church. She was quiet and shy in a way that made it hard for others to welcome her. Samantha guessed that her family probably didn't have as much money as most of the other families in their church. Emily came from a city more than a thousand miles from her new hometown, and everything about her seemed to shout "Different!" And nobody really liked her much, not even Samantha, who usually liked everybody.

When the sign-up sheet for winter retreat was passed around in Sunday school, everyone was encouraged to sign up in groups of four to be assigned to cabins. Samantha could see two or three other girls signalling to her from across the room, but Emily's downcast eyes nagged at Samantha's spirit and Samantha kept remembering a verse she'd read the morning before.

> *"Speak up for those who cannot speak for themselves,*
> *for the rights of all who are destitute.*
> *Speak up and judge fairly;*
> *defend the rights of the poor and needy."*
> *Proverbs 31:8-9*

Sticking Your Neck Out—for Love

Samantha being who she is, you can guess what she did. Would you have befriended Emily? Think about it, and be honest with yourself. Have you ever stuck your neck out for someone like Emily? How did it work out? Afterward, did you feel good about your choice?

The best example of selflessness we could ever have is Jesus Christ. Ask God to make you more and more like his Son in caring for the interests of others.

Do nothing out of selfish ambition or vain conceit, but in humility consider others better than yourselves. Each of you should look not only to your own interests, but also to the interests of others. Your attitude should be the same as that of Christ Jesus: Who, being in very nature God, did not consider equality with God something to be grasped, but made himself nothing, taking the very nature of a servant, being made in human likeness. And being found in appearance as a man, he humbled himself and became obedient to death—even death on a cross! Therefore God exalted him to the highest place and gave him the name that is above every name, that at the name of Jesus every knee should bow, in heaven and on earth and under the earth, and every tongue confess that Jesus Christ is Lord, to the glory of God the Father. Philippians 2:3-11*

■ Devotion #4: A Member of the Team

The following passages of Scripture revolve around spiritual gifts and the importance each child of God holds as a member of the "body." Encourage your

*Adapted from Annette Heinrich, One in a Zillion, *Shaw, 1990.*

children to see themselves as unique participants in a team effort. Help them to look for their particular talents and gifts and to find creative avenues for using them for Christ's kingdom.

Important Scripture Passages
Romans 12:3-8
1 Corinthians 12
Ephesians 4:1-16
Colossians 3:15-17

Wrapping It Up
The following devotional might be helpful in summarizing your Scripture reading of the past week, especially if your children are preschool and elementary-school aged.

Sleeping Beauty

Read a simplified version of the fairy tale "Sleeping Beauty," preferably one with colorful pictures. When the adventure is finished, let each child tell about his or her favorite part. Then draw the children's attention to the fairies who gave gifts to the princess when she was born (this could be the part *you* choose as your favorite part).

Each fairy gave a wonderful gift to the baby. One gave her beauty, one gave her music, and one gave her long life.

Of course, this is just a pretend story—a fairy tale. But something like that really happens when we are born into God's family. When we become Christians, God our heavenly Father gives us several gifts as he welcomes us to his family. First of all he gives us his Holy Spirit to live inside us forever and ever. All God's children receive that gift. But then God picks one or two very special gifts just for you. Some of his favorite gifts are the gift of teaching (so you can teach others to live for Jesus) and the gift of preaching (so you can preach and tell others about Jesus). Another special gift is the gift of helps. If you get that gift, you will love to do kind things for other people.

Wouldn't it be strange if we received a gift but never opened it and never used it? God does not want us to keep our gifts all wrapped up in their boxes. He wants us to unwrap them and share our gifts with our families and friends and people in our churches and neighborhoods.

When we use our gifts to help others, it is like giving a gift back to Jesus. How happy it makes him! (Suggestion: sing or play the song, "The Gift Goes On," sung by Sandi Patti.)

Questions to answer and talk about:
When do we get our special gift?
Who decides which gift we get?
What makes Jesus happy?
What gift do you think you would most like to have (preaching, teaching, helps, giving, encouraging, managing, etc.)?
If you had this gift, what would you do with it?

———

This devotional might be helpful in summarizing your Scripture reading of the past week if your children are older elementary or junior high aged.

One to Sow, One to Reap

Sherry lay across her friend Elena's bed, hugging the pillow and praying with all her might, "Lord, let her mom say yes!"

Elena was in the kitchen persuading her overprotective mom that summer camp would be a good experience for her. Sherry had spent the whole school year telling Elena about Jesus and about being a Christian. Elena had continued to put off making a decision to follow Jesus. Sherry really wanted Elena to come with her church group for a week at a Christian camp. And Elena really wanted to go, too.

Campfire Night

Five weeks later Sherry and Elena sat together on a log close to a campfire. It was the last night of a great week of summer camp. They'd gone swimming in the lake, practiced with bows and arrows, participated in small group devotions, taken trail rides on the camp horses, had a massive mud fight with the boys, listened to a great young people's speaker, kidnapped all the curling irons out of the other girls' cabins and held them for a ransom of M & Ms, learned to shoot real rifles, and made new friends.

Now it was Friday night. The next morning the whole group would pack up and go home. Campfire was a time for campers to sing together and to share what they'd been learning all week. Sherry almost fell off their log bench when Elena stood up to tell the whole group, "I accepted Christ this week!"

Glad Together

Elena explained that Janet, their camp counselor, had taken her aside three days before and talked with Elena about letting the Lord into her life. Elena had prayed with Janet to accept God's gift of salvation.

For just a moment, Sherry felt a twinge of envy. She had worked so hard to introduce her friend to Christ, and she had always imagined that she would be the one to help Elena make the decision. But Sherry was too full of gladness at having Elena as a sister in God's family to worry about that for long. She was just thankful that Janet was doing her part to serve the Lord.

God's Word explains that all the members of God's family share the work of spreading his kingdom. Jesus explained to his disciples about how one person might "sow" the seed of the truth, and another might "reap" it (John 4:34-38).

> *Just as each of us has one body with many members, and these members do not all have the same function, so in Christ we who are many form one body, and each member belongs to all the others. We have different gifts, according to the grace given us. Romans 12:4-6*

Even if you aren't around to see the good results, your efforts to serve the Lord are never wasted. Thank the Lord that you can be part of his serving team.

■ Devotion #5: Sharing God's Good News

Sharing the good news of salvation is an integral part of serving others for Jesus' sake. The following Scriptures include Christ's commands to "go into all the world." You and your children can share the goal of telling others about God's gift of salvation through Jesus.

Important Scripture Passages
Matthew 5:13-16
Matthew 28:16-20
Acts 1:8
Romans 1:16-17; 10:11-15; 15:14-21
2 Corinthians 5:17-21

Wrapping It Up
The following devotional might be helpful in summarizing your Scripture reading of the past week, especially if your children are preschool and elementary-school aged.

You Don't Have to Be Very Big at All

There's a fun and peppy chorus that goes like this:

> Oh, you don't have to be very big at all.
> Oh, you don't have to be very big at all!
> Jesus wants you for his helper,
> Whether big or small,
> And you don't have to be very big at all!

If you know that song, you can sing it right now. But even if you don't know the tune, the words help us think about something important: that God can use children as his helpers. Did you know that he has done exactly that many, many times?

Here are three short stories that are really true. Each story tells about a boy or girl who told other people about Jesus even though they were very small.

Story #1
Paulo was going on a long trip. His home was in Brazil, but he was traveling far away to the United States with his father and mother and brothers. Paulo was very excited. He had ridden the rivers of Brazil many times in small boats, but this time he would ride on a big ship. He would get to see a real ship's captain in his beautiful white cap and uniform.

Even as Paulo walked up the gangplank he could see the captain standing straight and tall on the deck. Paulo saluted as he passed—and the captain returned his salute!

Paulo liked the ship's captain very much. Whenever he could, he would talk to the captain like a friend, and the captain would talk to him.

One day the captain lit a cigarette and was smoking it by the rail when Paulo came by. "Mr. Captain," said Paulo, "It makes me sad to see you smoke. Smoking may make you sick and you may die. God made your body to be his temple. He wants to live inside of you. He wants you to love him and obey him."

"I will think about that, my little friend," said the captain. He smashed his cigarette and threw it into the sea.

Good for you, Paulo! You don't have to be very big at all!

Story #2

Louis Paul Lehman was just a little boy. When he became a Christian, God gave him the gift of preaching. Louis Paul did not wait until he grew up to use his gift, but he began to use it right away.

First Louis Paul preached in his own Sunday school to his friends. Then he was invited to go to other Sunday schools and churches to talk. Soon he was preaching in many churches in many places.

When all the people had gathered at the church, Louis Paul would tell them how Jesus could come into their hearts and live there.

All the time he was growing up, Louis Paul preached about Jesus. He kept right on preaching when he was a grown-up man. When he was a grandpa and God called him to heaven, he was right in the church he loved and where he had preached many times!

Good for you, Louis Paul. You don't have to be very big at all!

Story #3

Adele and Pooky were friends. They lived across the street from each other, so of course they played together. One sunny summer day they sat on the front porch while they cooled off with root beer popsicles.

Adele told Pooky that Jesus was God. She told Pooky that Jesus loved her and wanted her to love him. "I asked Jesus to come into my heart," Adele shared.

"When we ask him, he comes right in. Have you ever asked him to come in, Pooky?"

"No, but I want to," said Pooky. And she did, right then and there!

Good for you, Adele! You don't have to be very big at all!

Questions to answer and talk about:
Why did Paulo tell the ship's captain about Jesus?
Why did Louis Paul tell people about Jesus?
Why do you think Adele told Pooky about Jesus?
Can you think of someone you want to tell about Jesus?
What will you tell him or her?

Things to do:
Have a sing-along of choruses about witnessing: "This Little Light of Mine," "Give Me Oil in My Lamp," "Oh, You Don't Have to Be Very Big at All," "I Don't Have to Wait Until I'm Grown-up," and "Into My Heart."

Graph the ages of your family. On a long sheet of shelf paper, block out rows of one-inch squares for each member of your family. Each square represents one year of age. For example, you would color in three squares for the three-year-old, five for the kindergartener, thirty for Dad, etc. Use a different color for each family member. Put the names under each one's column. Post it for all to see.

———

This devotional might be helpful in summarizing your Scripture reading of the past week if your children are older elementary or junior high aged.

King of the Wimps

Max Taylor dipped a scratchy scrub brush into some sudsy water and started scrubbing bright red letters off the front of his gym locker. The disappearing words seemed to mock him: "GRANDMA TAYLOR," "BIBLE BANGER," "KING OF THE WIMPS."

His coach had met him at his locker, shaking his head sympathetically and saying, "There's no way to know who did it, Max, so I'm going to have to hold you responsible. I'll get the cleaning supplies, but I expect to see you here right after school."

Max knew who did it, though—at least, he could guess. Two weeks before, in English class, he'd ended up defending his belief in God in front of the whole class. He hadn't planned to tell so much, but when the teacher started talking as if believing in God were ridiculous, he just had to speak up. Four of the guys in that class were also in his gym class, and they'd spent the past two weeks experimenting with illegal tackles. Max knew they were out to get him, to make him angry enough to do what they would do: swear or hit back. So far, with God's help, Max had remained cool.

The graffiti on his locker was discouraging. "O.K., Lord," Max prayed while he scrubbed, "I'll even be king-of-the-wimps for you."

Out of This World

Three cheers and a slap on the back for Max Taylor! In God's eyes, Max is far from being king-of-the-wimps; he's a hero!

> *"If the world hates you, keep in mind that it hated me first. If you belonged to the world, it would love you as its own. As it is, you do not belong to the world, but I have chosen you out of the world. That is why the world hates you. . . . They will treat you this way because of my name, for they do not know the One who sent me." John 15:18-19, 21*

Christianity is not for wimps. Jesus knew it and told his disciples not to be surprised that the world would reject them, persecute them, and even kill many of them. God knows it's hard to be chosen "out of the world" and yet live right in it.

Muscle Building

To live courageously for Christ takes maturity, or spiritual muscles. Max's troubles with his English teacher and the guys in his gym class are like muscle-building exercises for his spiritual maturity. What experiences have you had that were spiritual muscle-builders?

> *Consider it pure joy, my brothers, whenever you face trials of many kinds, because you know that the testing of your faith develops perseverance. Perseverance must finish its work so that you may be mature and complete, not lacking anything. James 1:2-4*

It's difficult to think of hard experiences as "pure joy," but that's what God wants us to do. Pray that perseverance will finish its work in you, "so that you may be mature and complete."*

Expect God's Word to bear fruit in your child's life.
RITZ SCHWEITZ

---

*Adapted from Annette Heinrich, One in a Zillion, Shaw, 1990.

Learning as We Go Along
Section 4

The Teachable Moment

We teachers try to capitalize on what we call "the teachable moment." We keep our antennae operating to sense those special moments when a child's interest and curiosity are piqued by something happening just then. By using that person, that event, we can teach a related concept so that the child never forgets it.

Jesus himself was a master of this skill. Often he used examples, references to professions, articles of everyday life, and familiar situations to illustrate his points. A mustard seed, a lily of the field, a sparrow—Jesus looked for teachable moments and looked to his immediate surroundings for teaching tools.

Capturing the teachable moment is essential for teaching spiritual truths and values. For example, how can we teach a child not to steal, not to lie, not to covet? It's certainly difficult to plan ahead some field trip or fun activity that teaches these concepts.

Your best ally for teaching this kind of lesson—or any kind of lesson, for that matter—is the Deuteronomy 6 Principle. Deuteronomy 6:7 says, "You shall teach them [God's precepts] diligently to your children, and shall talk of them when you sit in your house, and when you walk by the way, and when you lie down, and when you rise" (RSV). Obviously, the Deuteronomy 6 Principle presumes that we spend time—a lot of time—with our children. The Principle is perfect for a summer schedule!

The Deuteronomy 6 Principle also presumes that we will be apt to teach (1 and 2 Timothy). We need to keep our minds set to the task of instructing our children and attuned to capture the teachable moment.

You might be thinking, "What?! With all these activities planned, who'll have time for anything else?" But as you carry out your calendar plans and as you set out on your adventures, your ministry or service visits, and your field trips, you'll discover you have all the time in the world to talk and to ask and answer questions.

At the zoo our family used to talk about habits of the animals, the countries they came from, and why the monkey screamed so loud at Brock.

At the beach we might discuss water safety and water plants and animals. What is seaweed? Do snails bite? How does sand get on the beach? Why does Dawn swim in a circle?

Everywhere we would exclaim over God's creative power, the variety of species he has made, and how he meets our needs through nature.

At the supermarket Marc and I talked about why I returned the money when a clerk gave me too much change.

And at home Adele discovered that my nose was red and my eyes wet just because I love Jesus and didn't ever want to drift away from him.

Most of us balk at being lectured. And like us, our children learn so easily, so happily when the lesson is a natural part of conversation, an answer to a question, or an overflow of our own hearts shared with them.

The following pages hold a few concepts and principles to teach by capturing some moment on some day when circumstance dictates (with the Lord's help). Once they're in your mind, you can teach them and others from God's Word as God arranges and prompts. Commit each day to the Lord. Ask him for many such teachable moments.

Learning Activities and Devotional Suggestions

Settling Summer Squabbles

We think you'll find that planning a calendar full of fun with a purpose will greatly cut down on the number of squabbles occurring on any given sunny summer day. As you give them your time and attention, challenge their thinking and skills, and turn their attention to think of God's presence and expectations, your children will be happier and more contented.

Still there may be fights over turf and terrain (especially when bedrooms are shared), infractions of the rules (inevitable in games), hurt feelings, or property tussles. They happen both inside the family and outside, with friends and neighbor children. So what then?

Teacher's tricks to the rescue again! But these tricks are based on solid scriptural instructions—which must be why they work so well!

Trying to teach the importance of strong interpersonal relationships and reconciliation isn't easy. A mental picture is always helpful when dealing with an abstract concept, so I have often given my students and children the following one by drawing it on the chalkboard or on a piece of paper.

Between you and every other person there is an invisible bridge of friendship. You can't see it with your eyes, but it stretches from your heart to theirs and from their mind to yours. As long as you remain a kind and thoughtful friend, your bridge will stay strong. But if you become selfish or speak unkind or untrue words to them or about them, then your bridge of friendship will be broken. You must never leave this bridge unrepaired. When you realize what you have done, you must take kind words with you and go to the one you have hurt. You must tell that person what you have done that is wrong, and you must ask that person to be your friend again. It is the only way to repair the bridge of friendship.

For example you can say, "I was wrong to call you a bad name and not let you have a turn. Will you be my friend again?" (Or, for older children, "Will you forgive me?")

When an argument has erupted and you are mediating, be sure not to allow the children to tell on each other. Assure one child that he will be heard in just a minute. Then ask the other what *he* himself did that was wrong. Then address the other child in the same way. Keep bringing each child back to his own part in the conflict, for children typically will lay the blame on someone else.

When each child has taken responsibility for what he has done, appeal to the conscience. Ask each child, "Was that the right thing to do?" Until children become accustomed to thinking this way on their own, it may be appropriate to ask each one, "How do you think so-and-so feels right now? Do you think he feels like being your friend?" Instruct the children to speak the actual words, "I was wrong to —" and to ask, "Will you be my friend again?"

A discussion of better ways to handle the original problem may be helpful. The goal is not just confession, not just assuming responsibility. The goal is restoration of the relationship—not a bad goal for us grown-ups, either.

It is heartwarming to see the ready forgiveness that children extend to one another. I have often seen two friends skip off together arm in arm within minutes of a nose-to-nose blow-up as if nothing had ever happened.

These steps to reconciliation restored the friendship completely.

So settling summer squabbles is part of "learning as we go along," because that moment of conflict between children is also "a teachable moment." In that circumstance, children are learning their responsibility to consider another's feelings or point of view. They are also learning to confront or confess or forgive. They are learning how to build and repair friendships. These lessons will serve them well—for a lifetime.

> **Life is full of interruptions,
> emergencies, crises, and urgent
> happenings. A mother must train
> herself to go with the flow.**
> **PAT HOLT AND GRACE KETTERMAN, M.D.**

Your Word Have I Hid in My Heart (Psalm 119:11)

When I (Joyce) was a little girl, I wanted to go to camp more than I had ever wanted anything. But with six brothers and sisters vying for the camp fund, it didn't look too promising—especially since I had my heart set on going for the full two weeks. But our church offered a way to earn money toward camp. For every Bible verse I learned, the church would apply some money to my savings for camp. Wow! What an opportunity! I began learning verses—and verses—and more verses. I practiced alone, then said them over and over to my long-suffering mother before repeating them word-perfect at church. No doubt the wise ones at church who designed the program knew—though I didn't—the tremendous influences those verses would have on my life.

It was these verses that taught me what was good and what was not and how to choose good over evil. They showed me that Jesus is the way to God and that his great desire is for me (and us all) to be one with him.

They gave me a standard for life—a guide for making life's choices—and gave me confidence. They taught me to trust God; they gave me glimpses into his character and ways, into the future, and even a sneak preview of heaven! They provided an introduction to Calvary and to Christ's sacrifice. Scripture brought me into conviction that I needed a different relationship with Jesus than I had experienced up until then. The Holy Spirit used these Scriptures to flood me with joy and confidence in the days that followed.

If ever there were an era when children need to be grounded in God's Word, it is this one. Children can't learn too much Scripture! Be sure to include a memorization program in your summer plans. You'll want to cooperate with any systems already in place to teach your child Scripture: Sunday school, Vacation Bible School, Five-Day Clubs. Encourage your children as they successfully complete their memory work. A midweek checkup may be helpful for children who are less motivated.

But you may want to enrich the established memory work with a plan of your own. You might adopt my church's plan and let your children earn their way to camp, verse by verse. Or you may choose verses that fit in with the summer devotionals in this book and learn them as a family. Charts and stickers (you can come up with others) are good incentives.

When my good friend Konnie was young, she learned whole chapters at a time. She and her brother earned new Bibles from Mom on completion of 500 verses learned word-perfect. What an excellent way to absorb Scripture in context!

Your local Christian bookstore should have Bible memory packets available, if you want extra help. Or you might choose your favorite verses and add them to the suggested list below. For the very young, Scripture songs make an effective memorization tool. In fact, singing Scripture helps anyone of any age to remember verses more easily.

Verses for Memorization

Genesis 1:1	John 15:7
Psalm 118:14	John 15:13
Psalm 119:11	John 15:17
Psalm 119:105	Romans 3:23
Proverbs 3:5-6	Romans 6:23
Matthew 5:13	1 Corinthians 13:4
Matthew 5:16	Galatians 5:22-23
Matthew 6:33	Ephesians 4:32
Matthew 8:27	Ephesians 6:7-8
Mark 12:31	Ephesians 6:12
John 1:11-12	Philippians 4:6
John 3:16	Philippians 4:13
John 14:1-3	Philippians 4:19
John 14:6	1 John 2:15-16
John 14:15	1 John 3:1-2
John 14:23	1 John 4:7-8
John 15:5	Revelation 3:20

Chapters for Memorization

Genesis 1	John 14
Exodus 20:1-20	John 15
Psalm 1	Romans 8
Psalm 23	1 Corinthians 13
Psalm 34	Galatians 5
Psalm 100	Ephesians 6
Psalm 103	1 Thessalonians 5
Psalm 145	Hebrews 11
Isaiah 53	1 John 3
Luke 2 (in 2 segments)	

Praying Together

Never is the teachable moment more valuable than in learning to pray together. It should not be an unusual experience in your home to gather everyone together for an instant prayer time for a specific need. Grandpa can't come to supper because he's down with a cold; Susan's cheerleading tryouts have been moved up to tomorrow; John needs a dark suit for choir and the cash flow is mighty low—"Let's pray right now" should be the byword.

As you pray together for needs inside and outside your immediate family, concern for other family members increases, joys and sorrows are commonly shared, and faith is built as God sends the answers to prayer.

But planned prayer sessions are also valuable and necessary. A creative approach breaks monotony. You might want to try some of these unique methods of praying for others.

A California pastor and his wife keep a 3 x 5 card file on their table with the church missionary families indexed inside. The children's names and ages are listed, as well as special needs for their specific work. Each day at breakfast, one missionary family is remembered in prayer. Then that card is rotated to the back of the file. In this way, the family shares a commitment to God's work in other countries and to their missionaries.

Another family we know keeps a box full of Christmas cards from the most-recent holiday season. At family prayer time, they choose a card and pray for that card-sender, focusing on specific needs and activities.

Friends in Illinois made a bright-colored prayer "chain." Strips of construction paper were marked with prayer concerns and looped into a long chain. During their after-dinner prayer time, they took down the chain from its decorative place in the dining room and each of the parents and five children prayed for a loop along the chain.

You'll want to be sure to incorporate prayer for one another in your family prayer times. Encourage your children to listen sensitively to one another's requests and to take turns praying out loud for each one. Having any group of people care for you by praying for you is helpful, but it is especially important for the family that hopes to grow in unity.

To back up your instruction on prayer with teaching from God's Word, choose some of the following Scriptures to use during a family devotional period.

Important Scripture Passages
Matthew 21:21-22; Mark 11:24
Ephesians 6:18-20
Philippians 4:6-7
Colossians 4:2-4
1 Thessalonians 5:16-18
1 Timothy 2:1-4, 8
James 5:13-16
1 John 5:14-15

Learning about the Trinity

One rainy afternoon when a mom was making homemade pretzels with her children, a question about the Trinity came up. That creative mom used the pretzels to illustrate the Trinity, twisting them so that the one long piece of dough overlapped into the traditional pretzel shape—with three "corners." No doubt her children had other questions about the roles of the Father, the Son, and the Holy Spirit, but the pretzel-making offered a simple way to illustrate "three in one."

"Trinity Pretzels" are a popular treat in that family. You might want to try pretzel-making with your own family. Try a pretzel recipe in your favorite cookbook or the following one.

Trinity Pretzels

1 pkg active dry yeast	½ tsp salt
1½ cups warm water	1 egg
3-4 cups of flour	1 Tbs cold water
2 tsp sugar	1-2 Tbs coarse salt

Dissolve yeast in warm water in a large bowl. Add sugar, salt, and 3 cups of the flour. Beat on low speed until moistened. Beat on medium about 3 minutes, scraping the bowl occasionally. Stir in more flour until dough is easy to handle.

On a lightly floured surface, knead dough until smooth and elastic, about 5 minutes. Place in greased bowl; turn greased side of dough up. Cover; let rise in warm place until doubled in size, about 1 hour. (Dough is ready if indentation remains when touched.)

Heat oven to 425. Punch down dough; divide in half. Cut each half into 6 equal pieces. Roll each piece into rope 15 inches long. Place rope on greased cookie sheet. Loop to form the pretzel shape. Enlarge space in the loops so they don't bake together. Place pretzels about 3 inches apart. Mix egg and cold water; brush over pretzels and sprinkle with coarse salt.

Bake until pretzels are brown, 15-20 minutes; cool on wire rack. Serve with mustard, if desired.

For Bible instruction on the Trinity, the clearest and most dramatic picture we have is found in Matthew 3:13-17, Mark 1:9-11, and Luke 3:21-22. This is the occasion of Jesus' baptism; all three members of the Godhead are clearly seen. God, the Son, is baptized. God, the Holy Spirit, lights on the Son's shoulders in the form of a dove. And God the Father's voice comes from heaven to bless and approve his Son.

To make the concept of the Trinity even more graphic, teach this episode from Jesus' life to your children using flannelgraph figures. Your church library may have a flannelgraph collection, or you might purchase it from a Christian bookstore or through Child Evangelism Fellowship.

Learning to Obey
By studying God's Word, children will learn that obedience is very important to the Lord—obedience to parents and other authority figures as well as to himself. Help your children commit themselves to obey God.

Important Scripture Passages

Joshua 22:5	John 14:15-21, 23-24
Psalm 103:17-18	Ephesians 6:1-3
Psalm 119:9-18, 97-105	Colossians 3:20
Proverbs 19:16	1 John 2:3-6; 3:21-24;
Jeremiah 7:23, 11:4	5:1-5
Luke 11:28	2 John 6

Wrapping It Up
The following devotional might be helpful in summarizing your Scripture reading of the past week, especially if your children are preschool and lower elementary-school aged.

What It Means to Obey
This short poem says a lot in a few words; we use it at Small World School for Young Children to help define the word "obey." We made up a simple tune for it so we could sing it with the children. You might do that, too, or simply learn the jingle together.

Do what I say,
Do it right away—
That's what it means to obey!

Make some "I Hear, I Obey" cards. You'll need:

4 x 6 cards
Colored markers or crayons

Brainstorm a list of fun commands, then write one command on each 4 x 6 card. Here are a few examples to get you started.
Jump 3 times
Twirl on one foot
Play "Mary Had a Little Lamb" on the piano
Do a somersault
Sing one chorus of "B-I-N-G-O"

Your family artist can illustrate the cards with cartoons or stick figures.

An older family member reads the commands, and each one in the family takes a turn obeying the commands. (Optional: you might want to use fish crackers, teddy grahams, or the like for a tiny, instant prize when anyone completes a command.)

Finish up with these questions and comments:

Could an army win a war if the soldiers didn't obey the general? What *would* happen?

Could a Little League team win if they didn't obey the rules of the game? What *would* happen?

Could Dad or Mom use the car if they didn't obey the driving laws? What *would* happen?

Rules and laws are made to keep people safe and healthy. They keep order in our schools and cities and country. It was God's idea to have law and order.

God has given us lots of rules to follow. They are written in the Bible. They are there to make us smart— so we know the very best way to live.

God wanted us to be happy and to have good lives. So he did not keep his rules a secret. He told us very plainly what to do and what not to do. If we do what God says, we will be healthy and happy. If we do not, we can be sure we will feel very bad and we will make God unhappy, too.

God has put dads and moms in charge of their children. When we obey our parents, it is just like we are obeying Jesus himself. So when Mom or Dad asks a favor of you or tells you to do something, remember this rhyme:

(Repeat together) Do what I say,
Do it right away—
That's what it means to obey.

———

This devotional might be helpful in summarizing your Scripture reading of the past week if your children are older elementary or junior high aged.

Sweating It Out

Sandy opened one eye and peeked out of the covers at the clock. 6:50—she had ten minutes before Mom would come to make her get up. The light sneaking around the corners of her windowshade and the warmth of Sandy's room told her that it was going to be a hot day. She rolled over and glared at her closet. The door was open, and some of her clothes (the rest were on the floor of the closet or in the hamper) were hanging there. *Ugh. The agony of dressing for school!*

Sandy had an old-fashioned mom—a mom who didn't think girls should wear shorts to school *ever*. Sandy had argued over and over again that all the girls did, that it wasn't against the rules, and that she would wear the longest ones she had—almost to her knees! But Mom never budged. And day after day, Sandy sweltered while her classmates could tan their legs at lunch time. Sandy thought about having it out with her mom again this morning. *I don't know which is worse, fighting with Mom or sweating at school.*

What Do You Think?
If Sandy were a friend of yours, what advice would you give her about dealing with her mom? Think through your answer carefully. Try to imagine how your solution would work in your own home.

Almost every young person disagrees with his or her parents some of the time. Can you think of a similar area of disagreement at your house?

Like it or not, your parents are the ones God gave you, and he had a purpose in choosing them for you. Obeying your parents even when it doesn't seem fair or logical not only keeps the peace at your house, it is obedient to God's Word.

> *Honor your father and mother, as the LORD your God has commanded you, so that you may live long and that it may go well with you in the land the LORD your God is giving you. Deuteronomy 5:16*

> *Children, obey your parents in the Lord, for this is right. "Honor your father and mother"— which is the first commandment with a promise—"that it may go well with you and that you may enjoy long life on the earth." Ephesians 6:1-3*

There's another good reason to obey your parents, and it's a reason we don't often think about: Obeying your parents is good training for obeying the Lord. There are going to be times in your life when doing things God's way seems unreasonable or even unfair, but God wants you to honor him with your obedience and wait to see what good things he will do with your choices.

Ask God right now to help you talk with your parents respectfully about things that seem unreasonable. Ask him to give you the courage to obey cheerfully even when things don't work out the way you'd like them to.*

All We Have Belongs to God

Summer provides older children the opportunity to pick up odd jobs. Even boys and girls not yet sixteen can mow lawns, walk dogs, deliver papers, and babysit.

When your children begin to earn their own money (or to receive a weekly allowance), it is time for them to learn biblical teaching on giving and then to practice setting aside part of that income for God's work in obedience to his instruction. Your children will need your help and oversight to get started.

Tipping or Tithing?

Even adults can fall into the short-sighted attitude of viewing a gift of money to the church or to Christian work as a "tip" to God—a reward to him for services rendered. Or, worse yet, they may see their gifts as a means of avoiding God's anger or buying his favor. The whole counsel of Scripture is needed to guide boys' and girls' thinking to understand that all we have belongs to God. We return a portion of it to him because he said that we should. We can understand the order because we care about the gospel being heard both at home and around the world. We know that his workers need to eat and live, and we know that people have needs that God wants to meet.

Adapted from Annette Heinrich, Not a Hollywood Family, Shaw, 1989.

Our own example will help our children see that giving—and so being God's partner—is a joyful experience!

Here are some Scriptures to help build these concepts.

How to Give:	Matthew 6:2-4
	1 Corinthians 16:2, 14
	2 Corinthians 9:6-7
	Colossians 3:17
How Not to Give:	Acts 5:1-11
Where Does Wealth Come From?:	Deuteronomy 8:18
	James 1:17
To What or Whom Should We Give?:	1 Corinthians 9:10-11
	1 Corinthians 16:1
	2 Corinthians 8:4, 14
	Philippians 4:14-16
	1 Timothy 5:17-18
How Much Should We Give?:	2 Corinthians 8:1-3
	Hebrews 7:5
Does God Reward Us for Giving?:	Malachi 3:10
	Luke 6:38
	Philippians 4:17-19
	Hebrews 6:10

A Tricky Task

Saturday morning commercials bombard children with images of Hawaiian Barbie, new comic-book or movie-hero toys, and the latest video games. It's as easy for them to want more as it is for us to sigh for a new dress, a new appliance, or a new car. It's important to keep uppermost in our minds that all we have is a gift from God and that we are to use what we have for his service. Keeping money and material things in perspective with our goals of spiritual maturity and heaven is tricky. Dig into God's Word again for help.

Important Scripture Passages
Matthew 5:42
Matthew 6:19-21, 24, 31-33
Philippians 4:19
1 Timothy 6:6-10, 17-19

Wrapping It Up
The following devotional might be helpful in summarizing your Scripture reading of the past week, especially if your children are preschool and elementary-school aged.

Mrs. Mafo's Miracle
(A true story from Africa)

(Have eight grains of rice ready to show the children during the story.)

Mr. Mafo was tall and strong and smart and kind. He lived far away in Africa with his wonderful wife and six cheerful children, Grandpa and Grandma, and several cousins and grandchildren.

Mr. Mafo had gone to college and now worked at a very good job. He got paid lots of money so he could feed his family and buy all the things they needed.

But Mr. Mafo felt sad. He saw that many of the people in his country did not know Jesus. And he had a good idea how to tell them about Jesus. But he did not have enough time to do his job *and* work on telling others about Jesus, too. What should he do? Mr. Mafo thought of what the Bible said: You can't serve God and money (Matthew 6:24). "That is true," said Mr. Mafo.

Then another thing the Bible said came into Mr. Mafo's mind: Give God first place in your life, and he will give you the other things you need (Matthew 6:33). Mr. Mafo decided to do what the Bible said.

So he quit his job and began the new job of telling other people about Jesus. Now Mr. Mafo was very happy. Mr. and Mrs. Mafo did not have as many extra tools and toys, but they remembered what God's Word said: Be content with food and clothes and what you have (1 Timothy 6:6-7, Hebrews 13:5). And so they were.

Soon a terrible drought came to their country. A drought is a time when the rain stops falling. If no rain falls for a long, long time, then no food can grow. The grass can't grow either; the lakes and ponds dry up, so of course the animals get too hungry and too thirsty, and then they die. That is just the kind of drought that came to where the Mafos lived. It was a terrible time; many people needed food. Many people needed water.

The Mafos needed these things, too. But they remembered what the Bible said. They remembered that God promised to get them all they needed (Philippians 4:19). So they prayed to their God, Jesus—and that was when the miracle happened.

That evening Mrs. Mafo made rice for supper. When everyone was full, there was still some rice left in the bowl. "This is not good," she said. "I must not waste any food since we need every bite we can get."

So the next night she did not put as much rice in the pot to boil. But when supper was over, what do you think? There was rice left over again! "Oh, dear," said Mrs. Mafo to Mr. Mafo. "I had better put even less rice on to cook next time." So she did.

Every night she put a little less rice and a little less rice in the pot, but every night there was rice left over again!

"This must be a gift from Jesus!" said Mrs. Mafo. That night she only put eight grains of rice in the pot, but it was enough to feed the six Mafo children, the Mafo grandma and grandpa, and all the cousins and grandchildren that lived there—and still there was rice left over!

All the Mafos knelt down and thanked Jesus for their rice and for his wonderful miracle. "Thank you, Jesus!" they said. "You are a great God. You are a God who keeps your promises. We love you!" they prayed, each and every one.

Questions to answer and talk about:
When Mr. Mafo had to choose between his job or telling others about Jesus, what helped him know what to do?
Why were the Mafos hungry and thirsty?
Who helped the Mafo family get the food they needed?
What promise did God make and keep in this story?
Does God give us what we need in the United States, too?

———

This devotional might be helpful in summarizing your Scripture reading of the past week if your children are older elementary or junior high aged.

Keep Out!

Ernie slipped the keys into the lock—doorknob and deadbolt. The door was plastered from top to bottom with signs reading, "STAY OUT," "TOP SECRET," "BEWARE OF MAD DOG," and "ENTER AT YOUR OWN RISK." It was Ernie's closet.

What do you think he kept in there? Not his clothes! No, Ernie's most important possessions were locked behind that door: the unbeatable matchbox car collection that he'd been working on since he was eight, the picture—which he'd sneaked from the yearbook office— of Melissa Sanderson (the most gorgeous and unattainable babe of his school), a baseball autographed by all the Chicago Cubs, six *Hot Rod* magazines, a huge

"EMERGENCY" sign he and his best friend had found next to a dumpster behind the hospital, twenty old issues of Spiderman comic books, a secret stash of Doritos and Twinkies, an empty beer bottle (he hadn't drunk it himself—he kept it just for show), four mushy letters from Allison (his girlfriend from the seventh grade), and the journals nobody knew he kept.

Ernie's closet was his treasure trove. He tried the handle before he went off to school. Anything to keep his little brother out!

Another Kind of Treasure
Do you have a secret stash somewhere of personal treasures? What are they, and where do you keep them?

There is a kind of treasure that can't be kept in a locked bedroom closet. There is a kind of wealth that people who don't follow Christ don't know anything about.

> *Command those who are rich in this present world not to be arrogant nor to put their hope in wealth, which is so uncertain, but to put their hope in God, who richly provides us with everything for our enjoyment. Command them to do good, to be rich in good deeds, and to be generous and willing to share. In this way they will lay up treasure for themselves as a firm foundation for the coming age, so that they may take hold of the life that is truly life.*
> *1 Timothy 6:17-19*

Rich in Good Deeds
In order to take hold of "life that is truly life," God wants us to be rich in good deeds. Talk about a time when you did something for God, something that would earn you a treasure stored in heaven.

Where Do You Keep Your Heart?
It's not wrong for Ernie to have a private place for his personal treasures—it's neat, and I hope his brother keeps out! But Ernie has another "treasure trove" kept in the storehouse of heaven.

> *"Do not lay up for yourselves treasures on earth, where moth and rust destroy, and where thieves break in and steal. But store up for yourselves treasures in heaven, where moth and rust do not destroy, and where thieves do not break in and steal. For where your treasure is, there your heart will be also." Matthew 6:19-21*

The matchbox cars, comic books, Twinkies, and old letters won't last forever, but Ernie's heart is with his treasure in heaven. Where do you keep your heart?*

**Of all the gifts that
a parent can give a child,
the gift of learning to make
good choices is the most valuable
and long-lasting.**
PAT HOLT AND
GRACE KETTERMAN, M.D.

A Goal of Godliness
As members of God's family, you and your children share a new goal and a new standard for living. The goal is godliness; the standard is Christ's holiness. Those are big challenges to strive for! Help your children understand God's commands to be "different" as part of his family and that holiness is God's choice for their lives.

*Adapted from Annette Heinrich, One in a Zillion, *Shaw, 1990.*

131

Important Scripture Passages

Psalm 1	1 Timothy 4:7-8
Romans 6:20-23	1 Timothy 6:6-12
2 Corinthians 6:16–7:1	Hebrews 12:14
Ephesians 1:4; 4:20–5:2	1 Peter 1:13-23; 2:2-10
Colossians 1:21-23	2 Peter 3:11
1 Thessalonians 4:1-8	

Wrapping It Up

The following devotional might be helpful in summarizing your Scripture reading of the past week, especially if your children are preschool and elementary-school aged.

Even a Child

Mindy is five years old. She has a new little sister. Mindy is angry because she didn't want a new baby to take her place. When her mom isn't looking, Mindy reaches into the crib and pinches the baby.

Stormy's dad is not a Christian. When his dad is at work, Stormy sneaks his bad magazines to a secret place and looks at the pictures.

Jill is lazy and sometimes just pretends to wash her hands or brush her teeth instead of really doing these things. When Mom asks, "Did you brush your teeth?" or "Did you wash your hands?" Jill tells her mom "Yes."

When God sees Mindy and Stormy and Jill doing these things, do you think he says to himself, "That's O.K. They are just little boys and girls. Someday they may do better"?

No, indeed! In the Bible it says that God wants children to do right even when they are young. God says, "Even a child is known by his actions, by whether his conduct is pure and right" (Proverbs 20:11).

When we get an idea to do something naughty, we must holler to God for help—right away! Just like we run to dial 911 for emergency help, we must pray to Jesus and say, "Please help that bad idea to go away. Please help me to obey."

Then run to Mom or Dad for a hug—or get busy doing something fun or useful. God will answer your prayer!

Questions to answer and talk about:
Do you think that Mindy and Stormy and Jill know they are doing wrong things? How do they know?
How do you feel when you do something bad?
What two things should we do when we get a bad idea?
If we do sin (do something bad), how do we make it right with God?

———

This devotional might be helpful in summarizing your Scripture reading of the past week if your children are older elementary or junior high aged.

Why Be Normal?

Valerie dipped a French fry into her chocolate shake, then popped it into her mouth.

"Disgusting!" said her sister Connie, making a face. "You've been doing that since you were two years old. When are you going to grow up and eat ketchup like normal people?"

"Why be normal?" asked Valerie, laughing.

Connie smiled, too. She and Val had been saying, "Why be normal?" to each other for years.

When Val's friends criticized her Saturday visits to the retirement center as different from their shopping trips at the mall, Connie told her, "Who cares what they say? Why be normal, anyway?"

When Connie felt pressured by the other girls on the pep squad to go to a party where there was lots of drinking, Val encouraged her not to feel bad about being different: "Why be normal?"

And when friends at a slumber party teased them that they were probably the only girls in school who hadn't gone "all the way," Val and Connie laughed and said, "Why be normal!?"

Who Makes the Rules?
Who makes the rules for "normal" anyway? Just because everybody is doing something doesn't make it right or wise. When Val and Connie became members of God's family, they accepted a new standard for "normal," a standard of holiness.

> *As obedient children, do not conform to the evil desires you had when you lived in ignorance. But just as he who called you is holy, so be holy in all you do; for it is written: "Be holy, because I am holy" ... You are a chosen people, a royal priesthood, a holy nation, a people belonging to God, that you may declare the praises of him who called you out of darkness into his wonderful light. 1 Peter 1:14-16; 2:9*

We've Got Each Other
Val and Connie are lucky to have each other's support for standing firm in what they believe. Val and Connie have "fellowship."

> *As iron sharpens iron, so one man sharpens another. Proverbs 27:17*

> *Two are better than one, because they have a good return for their work: If one falls down, his friend can help him up. But pity the man who falls and has no one to help him up! Ecclesiastes 4:9-10*

Do you have a "fellowship" type of friend? Maybe it's your mom or dad, or maybe a brother or sister. How do you "sharpen" each other? How do you help each other up?

Thank God for your friends or family members who help you stand up for your goal of godliness. Ask God to help you live by his holy standard for "normal."*

Ruling an Unruly Tongue

You've probably done battle for the control of your own words, so you know how important it is for children to begin to see how important their words are. Words can build up or tear down; words can praise or criticize; words can hurt or heal. The Scriptures have a lot to say on the subject of ruling an unruly tongue. Lead your children on an investigation of God's teaching about controlling our words.

Important Scripture Passages

Psalm 19:14; 39:1; 141:3
Proverbs 10:11-13, 18-21
Proverbs 12:13-25
Proverbs 15:1-4, 23
Proverbs 16:23-24
Proverbs 25:11

Proverbs 27:2
Ephesians 4:29-30; 5:19-20
Colossians 3:8-10
James 1:26; 3:2-12

Wrapping It Up

The following devotional might be helpful in summarizing your Scripture reading of the past week, especially if your children are preschool and lower elementary-school aged.

Nasty Pup

Once upon a time there was a naughty, nasty pup. He barked and he bit and he chewed the carpet up.

Adapted from Annette Heinrich, One in a Zillion, Shaw, 1990.

His owner bought a muzzle and locked it on his head.
Then the dog wished he'd always kept his mouth shut
    instead!

Once upon a time there was a naughty, nasty tongue.
It lied and it teased and its hurting words all stung.
Its owner read the Bible, which said, "It's wrong to
    lie!"
Now the tongue sings nice songs and does not make
    others cry!

If your tongue will not mind you and says some
    naughty thing,
Get down upon your knees; talk about it to the King.
He made your tongue, he made your heart, and he
    can fix it so
Your tongue will have a muzzle to help it stop and
    go.

Loving words and kind words will always be the rule.
Soft words and helpful words—never harsh or cruel.
True words and thoughtful words build a friendship
    up.
I'd rather wear God's muzzle than be a nasty pup!

Things to Do to Control an Unruly Tongue:
1. Learn Psalm 39:1a:
    "I said, I will guard my ways,
    That I may not sin with my tongue;
    I will guard my mouth as with a muzzle."
    Psalm 39:1a (NASB)

2. Brainstorm do's and don'ts for tongues. Write your
list with a marker on a long sheet of shelf paper. Tack
it up as a reminder for a week or two.

For Fun

Make a Munchie Mouth. You will need:

2 apple slices with the skins on (lips)

peanut butter (gums)

miniature marshmallows (teeth)

Put a generous amount of peanut butter on one side of each apple slice. Line up the marshmallows close together in the peanut butter on one apple slice. Then lay the other apple slice on top of the teeth. Gently pinch the backs of the apple slices together. All finished! You should see a toothy smile. Smile back!

———

This devotional might be helpful in summarizing your Scripture reading of the past week if your children are older elementary or junior high aged.

Big Mouth

Serena had a big mouth. She knew it, and she was sorry about it. Night after night she'd go to bed realizing that she'd blown it again: criticizing her brother's computerized windmill science project, slipping her sister's secret into Mom's ear, or hogging all the conversation at dinner.

Why didn't all her resolutions and good intentions work?!

Serena's Strategy

Serena finally talked with her mom about the problem, and her mom suggested that she read the book of Proverbs and copy all the verses that refer to the tongue or talking.

This is ridiculous, thought Serena once she got started. *There must be a hundred of these!*

There were so many it took Serena nearly a month to finish the project. These are a few of the verses she wrote down:

> *The tongue that brings healing is a tree of life.*
> *Proverbs 15:4a*

> *A man finds joy in giving an apt reply—*
> *and how good is a timely word!*
> *Proverbs 15:23*

> *A wise man's heart guides his mouth,*
> *and his lips promote instruction.*
> *Pleasant words are a honeycomb,*
> *sweet to the soul and healing to the bones.*
> *Proverbs 16:23-24*

Curse or Blessing?

Pretty soon Serena started to realize that with some self-control and the help of the Holy Spirit, her big-mouth curse could actually become a blessing.

Her infamous gift of gab was useful for keeping her bedridden grandpa company.

She discovered that she could be a great friend to shy people.

Her creative ability for clever put-downs against her sister and brother was really just the flip side of a creative ability to encourage and build up others. It became a challenge—and a sharpening skill—always to find something nice to say.

> *With the tongue we praise our Lord and Father,*
> *and with it we curse men, who have been made*
> *in God's likeness. Out of the same mouth come*
> *praise and cursing. My brothers, this should*
> *not be. Can both fresh water and salt water*
> *flow from the same spring? James 3:9-11*

That's the Way God Made Her

After all, who gave Serena her motor mouth? God did! And he was just waiting for Serena to dig into his Word to discover how to use her "gift" for his kingdom.

In your head think of each person in your family. Now think of one nice or praiseworthy thing about that person.

Do you have a "gift" that can be both a curse and a blessing? Think of some ideas for how you might use that gift to please God.

Ask God to help you communicate your encouraging words to your family today. (Sometimes this is very difficult!) Ask him to teach you through his Word how to use all your gifts for him.*

*Adapted from Annette Heinrich, Not a Hollywood Family, Shaw, 1989.

A Fantastic Family Vacation– at Home or Away

Section 5

Making Time for an Adventure

Many of our favorite memories are connected with family trips—not always a standard "vacation," but a trip to Grandma's, or a ministry fundraising trip, or a cross-country move. Certain hymns always remind me (Annette) of our family because we often sang them in the car. The mere mention of Dramamine conjures up more mental pictures than I want to remember! And all roadmaps bring back a memory of learning to calculate for myself how long it would be until we "got there."

Planning a special, concentrated time for family togetherness can be exciting for the whole family. Each family member can contribute activity ideas and share in the anticipation of that enjoyable time.

Perhaps a week-long family vacation is out of the question for your family this year—as it often was for our family. Perhaps work schedules or finances won't permit that time away from home. You can set aside "Camp Week" or "Vacation Week" for your family at home by turning the usual work and service and play routines upside down and replacing them with a camp schedule and camp activities.

This chapter of the book includes two **Learning Activities** sections—one for the family road trip and one for the family vacationing at home. The **Devotional Suggestions** will cover one week of special devotions surrounding the theme of "God Is So Great!"

We hope your family will have time for at least a short "retreat" from the ordinary, and that you will grow together as you share fun and learning experiences.

We can't restore childhood once it's gone, but we can make a commitment to it when it's in our grasp.
JOAN RAE MILLS

Learning Activities for Travel

No matter where you choose to go on your family vacation, we want to help fill the hours of travel time or hotel time with activities that build togetherness. You might want to incorporate some of these into your car trip.

Before You Leave

Since anticipation is a good part of the fun, start enjoying your vacation before you leave. Gather as much information as you can about your destination.

A trip to your local library will provide a wealth of information. Encyclopedias furnish facts on the weather, geography, topography, and history. There may be a whole book devoted to the state or site that you have chosen to visit.

You could send for brochures from the State Department of Tourism (addresses available from the library). In these you'll find pictures and thumbnail sketches of the area's best points of interest that you may want to include in your itinerary. Famous mansions, homes of historic figures, caves, and museums hold interest for family members of almost any age.

Find out what the local industries are, then plan to include a trip to the cranberry bog, wild rice field, strawberry patch, cherry orchard, dairy farm, cattle ranch, oil refinery, mint, woolens factory, fish hatchery, etc.

Get maps of the areas between home and your destination, then plot your course with colored highlighters. Be sure to mark the spots you will stop to see.

At least two or three days ahead, lay out the suitcases. With some guidelines, allow the children to pack their own clothes. Help them think through how long they will be gone, the climate where they are going, and the kinds of special clothes they'll need for activities.

If the trip is a long one and funds permit, you may want to borrow an idea used by friends of ours, who say it was a great hit! Mom made a "gift chain." She tied small, individually wrapped presents together with colored yarn in a long chain. The children took turns opening them—one in the morning, one in the afternoon—knowing that their prizes were for sharing with other family members. This mom chose items suited for travel fun: coloring books, sticker books, colored pencils, a bag of orange slices, small cars and planes, cellophane tape, storybooks, and audio tapes. You can probably come up with ideas of your own, some of them suited to your children's special interests. Maybe all your children would like to be involved in buying and wrapping one or two contributions to the gift chain.

Don't forget to mark the vacation dates on your Summer Calendar. Mark the dates when you will leave, when you come home, and perhaps some highlights in between.

And *just* before you leave, bow your heads together and ask Jesus for his blessing and help and protection.

What to Take in the Car

Since Dad was the primary driver, Mom (Joyce) typically had the job of keeping the five of us occupied—in other words, to distract us from jabbing one another with elbows, arguing over the window seats, or giving our little brother snuggies (pulling up his underwear as far as it would go). Mom had a large cloth bag that went along on every trip and was almost as important as her purse. It had to be packed right at her feet on the passenger side. In it she kept the tools of her entertainment trade. Here are a few suggestions for a Mom's Travel Bag:

Songbooks or songsheets
Lots of paper and pencils
Maps, atlases
Travel games: Who Am I? Bible Cards, Travel Bingo, any hand-held electronic games (that don't annoy the driver!)
Books
Dramamine, paper lunch sacks, a damp cloth, and handtowels (for travel disasters)
Jumprope, nerf football, frisbee, or other toys for travel stops
Small Walkman stereo set with headphones and favorite cassettes

It might be a good idea to allow each of your children to carry his own car-travel bag, complete with the toys and games he likes best—matchbox cars, paper dolls, a sticker book, small craft sets with yarn or embroidery floss, etc.

Imagination Magic

One of your best tools to keep the troops entertained is imagination magic. Use your creative thinking to make the places you go more interesting.

Dad, mom, or older children can reach back for the near-forgotten facts of history and tell the stories of heroes, heroines, and legendary figures that have populated the region in which you find yourself. For example:

Paul Bunyan and Babe
Davy Crockett
Harriet Tubman
Babe Ruth

Sitting Bull
Clara Barton
Billy the Kid
Annie Oakley
Billy Sunday
Johnny Appleseed

The list is endless! As the stories unfold, one can almost imagine Johnny planting his seeds, or Babe smacking that ball out of the park one more time.

It's always worth an early start to catch a sunrise or to explore the beach at low tide! Use your imagination!

Our family always made a special moment of "The Hour of the Silhouettes," or dusk, when the sun is barely down and all the trees and houses look like silhouette cutouts across the landscape. A sense of anticipation would fall on us when one would remind the others, "It's almost the Hour of the Silhouettes!" We would all watch out the windows, hushed at the drama of descending darkness.

Round-the-Car Storytelling

At home after dinner Dad often would take time to tell us a story—usually what we called an "Abner Story" because he created the tales around the character of a Texas farm boy named Abner, who had a sister Sally and a horse of his own named Blackie. But as we got a little older and as Dad's store of good tales was nearly exhausted, he created a new tradition. Dad would start the story and then stop at a crucial turning point in a story and pass the tale to one of us. The next storyteller could take the tale in any direction he chose, so that between seven storytellers we often spun a tale that included spaceships, pirates, sharks, farmers, princesses, and soldiers.

This style of storytelling is very entertaining and most adaptable for use during car travel. If you have a smaller family—and therefore fewer storytellers—you may want to go around two or even three times before your tale is completed. The more creative, outlandish, and silly, the better!

If your family comes up with a really exceptional round-the-car story, you might want to put it on paper—as a memento of your trip.

Stop Early

Our friends in Wheaton, Illinois, the Taylcrs, have five children in their family, and every summer they make a family trip around an annual conference that Mr. Taylor attends. Mrs. Taylor has learned that her children handle the car trip better if they get a good chance to enjoy the unusual pleasure of the hotel stay. So even though you might drive long days and stop late to sleep if you were on your own, stop early enough in the day for your children to enjoy the pool and whatever other facilities your stopping place affords.

The same idea holds true for campsites, if you are camping as you travel. Children will especially enjoy exploring their surroundings if there are some daylight hours allotted for that purpose.

When one cross-country move took us through Yellowstone National Park, Dad made a special point of pulling over just before we entered that great preserve. It was five in the morning. He woke everyone up because he didn't want us to miss seeing any wildlife that might be moving around at that hour. We strained our eyes to scan the landscape—and we were not disappointed. Five or six moose thundered across the road right in front of the car. We saw elk and bears and deer, and it was better than a trip to the zoo anywhere, anytime!

Are We There Yet?

It's a question we've all heard—too often. It's difficult for children to be patient with car travel, especially when it's hard for them to measure time as it passes.

I remember Mom and Dad helping me (Annette) learn to read the family's atlas. I felt important when Dad would pass it to me from the driver's seat and say, "Will you figure out about how many miles it is from Madison to Chicago for me?" I'd use my finger or a pencil to measure against the map's mileage guide and figure it out for myself.

One family magazine offered this travel tip: provide older children with a pocket atlas and a highlighting marker. The children could mark their destination with a star and then measure their progress from city to city.

One-on-One

Long car-travel hours can provide the opportunity for a parent to spend some one-on-one time with a child. Of course, the rest of the family is within earshot—but when you and one child are engrossed in a game or a puzzle, the others will quickly put their noses into their own books or games. Even without complete privacy, this one-on-one time builds relationship.

Mom (Joyce) would often move to the backseat to spend some time with us kids and to give another child a chance to ride in the coveted "front-seat" space. I remember Mom playing endless rounds of "Go Fish" with Brock. She played "Battleship" with Marc. With me, it was "Hang-man." Both of us enjoyed—and still do enjoy—word games. We'd take turns coming up with tricky names or phrases, drawing out the spaces and the gallows, and taking guesses from the alphabet. I have to admit she got me on "Xavier Cugat." To this day, I don't know who that is, though Mom insists he is famous.

A friend of ours used a car trip with her preadolescent daughter to listen to and discuss Dr. James Dobson's "Preparing for Adolescence" series. She claimed her audience was "captive," and the length of the car trip allowed for time to become comfortable talking about personal subjects. This, of course, would not be appropriate with all the family members in the car.

If you are a single parent and will be the only driver, your one-on-one times will have to be shared with the child taking his turn in the passenger seat. Be sure to rotate seating positions so every child gets his chance to have special time with you.

I (Annette) have never been much of a car sleeper. I was always envious of my sister Dawn, who practically falls asleep the moment the wheels hit the freeway. Dad liked to drive at night—probably because it was quieter with the five of us children asleep and because sleeping children require fewer potty stops. Mom has difficulty staying awake at night, so I, the wide-awake one, was often the designated company to keep the driver awake. I still remember Dad telling me stories of his childhood, of his time in Korea, or of times that I was too little to remember. Those were good times of growing relationship for me and Dad.

Yes, the long hours of cooped-up car travel can be stiffening and wearying (and can make you sigh with the thought of yet another burger and fries), but the time spent with your children will be a valuable and lasting "side effect."

Alphabet Game
The alphabet game involves scanning the billboards and license plates as you drive along the freeway, hunting out "A, B, C" and so on as you drive. The letters must be scouted out in order—a "Q" that is found before a "P"

can't be counted. The object of the game is, of course, to find all the letters in order, A-Z.

This is a game for one or for many. It's a good way to help a car-sick child look out the window and forget about his stomach. Even if he cannot read, a child who knows the alphabet can watch for the letters. Two children or two groups can play—each taking a side of the road. One group scans for letters out the left windows, and the other out the right.

Sing a Song

Our family sang so often on cross-country trips that to this day there are certain songs that immediately remind me (Annette) of car travel. Some were hymns like "How Great Thou Art" and "Heaven Came Down and Glory Filled My Soul." Others were silly sing-along songs like "I'm in Love with the Garbage Man's Daughter," "Dirty Bill," and "I Love the Flowers, I Love the Daffodils." The choices of songs to sing reflected the different ages and personalities of all the members of our family. I remember Marc teaching the rest of us kids songs he'd learned at summer camp—songs I'm sure Mom would have loved to leave out of our repertoire!

Our cousins made up a song to fit with any family member's name in order to "salute" that family member for something he or she did, like offering to wash the windows at a stop or to pump the gas, or to get Mom a cold drink. For a type of three cheers for the good-deed-doer, the rest of the family would all sing:

Hooray for Patty!
Hooray for Patty!
Kind and wonderful and cute,
Good and brilliant and astute.
Hooray for Patty!
Hooray for Patty!
She's the best window-washer of all!

If you can pick out the tune on an instrument, here are the notes:

```
C  F  G  A  C
C  F  G  A  C
A  Bb  A  G  G  F#  G
G  A  G  F  F  E  F
C  F  G  A  C
C  F  G  A  C
A  Bb  A  G  C  A  F
```

You might find occasions to affirm each family member with this song during your trip.

You might want to pack along a favorite songbook or hymnal. Be sure to let each family member make song requests.

Read a Book

You will want to pack in-the-car reading for each of your children. But if your family is anything like ours, there will be some members who are unable to read in the car because of motion sickness. If you or one of the older children are able, choose a book to read aloud in the car together as a family.

We've found that books on cassette are also enjoyable—for parents and kids. These are available in bookstores and libraries.

As your children read the books they packed for their private reading, you might ask them to "report" now and then about how they like the book, or what exciting things are happening in the story. One child's report on a story adventure may develop another child's interest in reading that book.

You might want to set aside twenty minutes of travel time for family devotions and family prayer. You could use the suggested devotionals in this chapter, or prepare others you feel are appropriate to your family's growth this summer.

Home Again, Home Again

Coming home can be *almost* as exciting as going in the first place! If your pets have been left behind, there's a happy reunion for both children and animals on arrival. And neighborhood playmates will no doubt be anxious for your return. It's joyful to see old friends again and to sort through the huge pile of accumulated mail.

But before the memories of your vacation fade away, capture some of those special moments by making a family scrapbook of the trip. Include in your book all the notes, brochures, and maps you collected before the trip. Along the way, buy postcards of scenes that typify the areas or places you all especially loved and enjoyed. These can be put into the scrapbook with captions and comments. Keep fliers and mementos from museums and other sites visited to be glued or taped in place. And any snapshots you take yourself are a great addition.

Have each family member journal his or her memories and most meaningful experiences. Even pre-schoolers can tell about their favorite fun times while an older brother or sister writes down their words for them. Conclude your book with these.

Keep the scrapbook in an accessible spot in the family room for all to enjoy over the long winter months.

Not all vacations turn out perfect and wonderful! Sometimes you'll wonder if you really do want to remember them at all—like the trip we took that included a wild sandstorm in Wyoming, which sifted grit through every crevice of our moving van. Each drawer, every box, everything we owned had to be washed, cleaned, or polished on arrival.

Or the time when the air conditioner failed in 100+ heat as we crossed the salt flats of Utah. The glue holding the interior lining of the station wagon dried, and wide strips of cloth fell and dangled in our faces. We all baked dry at those temperatures, and we sat silently sucking on ice cubes from the not-so-cool cooler. Sugar, our huge and hairy dog, drooled from the back down the children's necks. Ugh—what a memory!

Our friends the Hedlunds just shared that their latest vacation was a near disaster. They had major car trouble, Laurie landed in the hospital, and Grandpa wanted to go home NOW and said so repeatedly! But, they say, it still turned into a wonderful time because of prayer and God's very immediate help in time of trouble. Laurie's problem turned out to be treatable and short-lived. God had provided extra money before the trip; it was enough to cover the cost of the car breakdown. And because they were "grounded" without wheels, they got lots of rest and enjoyed a unique time of family sharing and fun just by being together.

Prayer, faith in the Father, praise for his help, and a sense of humor can save the day!

We had one terrible moment when a huge truck had missed our car by a hair's breadth because its wheel loosened and rolled down the road in another direction. We sat in stunned silence after Dad had slammed the car to a stop at the side of the road. Our youngest brother, Brock, broke the tension by piping up with his version of the old country-music song about "Lucille": "You picked a fine time to leave me, Loose Wheel!" he sang.

Keep laughing. Keep praying. Keep praising the Lord! You can keep your perspective and make any vacation a great one to remember.

Learning Activities for a Home Vacation

Your family probably will not be able to take a vacation away from home every summer. But if your own schedule permits, set aside a week for "Camp" at home, preparing to include various activities that are characteristic of a camp setting and completely outside the everyday routine. We hope the following activity suggestions will help make your vacation at home a week to remember.

Camp Schedule

A week at summer camp would include daily devotional time with the counselor (that's you!), sports, scheduled special activities, a week-long craft project, and perhaps an occasional pillow fight. So, for this one week of the summer, relax your summer work schedule to its minimum—perhaps only making beds, light bathroom clean-up, and kitchen duty—to allow time for Camp activities.

Try to stick with a day-camp routine. A sample is included here.

7:00   Bugle wake-up for one and all (no TV cartoons this week!). Time for dressing, getting chores out of the way. (Can someone in the family play reveille on a trumpet? Great! If not, have a friend who can tape it so you can blast it through the house in the morning.)

7:30   Camp calisthenics. Pick an older child to be in charge of leading thei·, or take turns with several older children. Hunt up a real gym whistle for this event!

7:45   Camp breakfast. Be sure to eat together as a family, even if this is not part of your normal schedule. Use paper plates, etc. to cut clean-up time. On the morning you make pancakes, try some wild animal shapes. A circle with two small circles on top makes a bear-face. A triangle with antlers drizzled on top makes a deer. A U-shape with a thick scalloped antler on top makes a moose. You and your kids will think of others.

8:00   Camp lunch preparations. All work together to prepare a picnic lunch.

8:15   Special Camp Week Activity (a family outing or field trip).

12:00 Lunch. Find a nearby park or forest area to picnic.

1:00 . Camp daily devotions. Use the material suggested in this chapter, or select topics and passages that correspond to chosen activities or the needs of your children.*

*For more camp ideas, take a look at Shaw Discovery Guides for Campers. Each guide includes one week of interactive Bible studies, reinforcing activities, and Scripture memorization—all integrated in one theme—and is easily adaptable for home use. Twelve different guides for juniors and teens are available at your local bookstore or from Harold Shaw Publishers.

1:30   Craft hour. Working together, allow children to work on personal craft projects.

2:30   Afternoon Sports Activity. Have a family softball game or frisbee contest. Go together to swim at a local public pool or lake. Or find a stable that offers a trail ride. (You may want to select an activity that is less strenuous if your morning outing was rigorous.)

4:30   Free time.

5:30   Dinner.

6:00   Fun together as a family. Rent a movie and eat popcorn. Have a campfire (Some friends make a campfire in their Weber Kettle! More campfire ideas on page 11.) Have a puzzle night—or a night of table games (especially good for a rainy evening). Be creative!

9:30   Lights out. Sound "Taps" by your trumpeter or your tape. Mom and/or Dad sing a good-night song to all campers. (Some ideas: "Good Night, Our God Is Watching over You," "Now It's Time to Rest, like Robins in Their Nest," or "If I Have Wounded Any Soul Today.") Have a Waltons' family type of good-night, with each family member saying a loud good-night to every other family member by name.

Your camp schedule may include suppertime barbecues, or other unique evening activities. The purpose of the schedule is to provide a framework for the week, but the name of the game is FUN. So be flexible with your camp schedule!

Animals

Every camp has horses or dogs or other animals. If possible, include animals in your camp-week, whether by a trip to a local farm, petting zoo, or trail-ride stable. One little girl I know is perfectly delighted just to go to the local animal shelter to visit all the kittens and puppies that need love there. (This, however, can be dangerous unless you are looking for a new pet!)

Crafts

Some day-camp programs allow children to spend part of each day working on a handcraft project to be completed by the last day of camp. A walk through the children's craft aisles of your local toy store will spark some ideas. You might also check out the Vacation Bible School materials at the Christian bookstore; these typically include week-long craft ideas.

It's a good idea to allow your children to choose the craft of their interest; children are more apt to begin and stick with a project of their own choosing. Perhaps your older son wants to build a model of the Starship Enterprise from "Star Trek." Or perhaps your daughter has been asking you to teach her to embroider or crochet. Children of any age enjoy clay, and younger children love to build with Legos.

Some other simple suggestions are soap carving (Ivory is soft and usually very inexpensive), carving a potato into a shape for printing with an ink pad, creating puppets from paper lunchsacks or stray socks, or putting together collages from magazine cut-outs. You may want to concentrate on nature crafts, using shells, seeds, bark, or twigs.

A time set aside for handiwork is a good way of incorporating some relatively "quiet" time for your children in the midst of a busy camp schedule. While their hands are busy with projects, your children may still enjoy positive interaction with one another.

Family Field Trips

You already know all about family field trips. Be sure to incorporate one or two in this special week of "camp."

You might want to start a tradition for camp week. One family attends an annual sand sculpture contest in their community. If your community doesn't offer something like this, have a sand sculpting contest of your own.

Other fun family summertime activities might include berry picking, fishing, tree climbing, shell collecting, etc.

Dad used to pile us all in the car on a summer evening and take us on a "Penny-flip ride." When we came to an intersection, we flipped the coin—heads we turned right, tails we turned left. On foot or in the car, you might take a penny-flip adventure. Somehow, when Dad took us, we usually ended up at Dairy Queen!

Again, your children are a wonderful resource for field trip ideas—take time to find out what they've always wanted to do or to see.

Exploring Your Camp

Even if you've lived in your town for a long time, you may never have taken time to go "exploring." What are the interesting or fun highlights near your home that you've never taken time to visit?

I (Annette) lived in Wheaton five years before I ever took a long walk straight west from the main residential area. There was interesting swampy ground there that would delight any young explorer. When my roommate and I got a dog, I discovered open spaces that had been right under my nose, but I hadn't even noticed them until I had a real reason to go out exploring. Last summer my husband's small cousins and I had a lovely long walk outdoors with three baggies and a children's book about types of leaves. We had an hour's adventure as three scientific explorers.

Take some time this week to discover something new about "the same old place."

The Last Night of Camp Week

Make the last night of Camp Week something really spectacular. Perhaps this is the best night for a family campfire, taking time to share what each family member liked best about the vacation at home. Perhaps this is a good night for camping out in the yard or sleeping on the floor in sleeping bags.

One year, on the very last day of summer before school began again, Mom gave us a day off from the regular work schedule and made us a kooky lunch—the backward lunch. You surely recognize the age-old struggle between moms and kids about junk food. Kids love it; moms hate it. Just this once, Mom made a celebration lunch full of goodies. She told us we were having soup and crackers, then served us chocolate pudding in the soup bowls, with cookies alongside! We were astonished. It never happened again, but it was something we never forgot! A backward lunch may be in order for your last official day of camp.

Another idea, for camp week or another time, is for your family to plan a theme party. You might allow each family member to invite two or three friends, or invite two or three other families. For example, if your family can't afford a real Hawaiian vacation, have a luau in the back yard! Or plan a 20s or 50s party, complete with creative costumes.

Make the last night of Camp Week a night to live on in the memories of your family's togetherness.

Devotional Suggestions

If your family is making a specific trip to the mountains or the ocean, you might want to tailor your family devotion times to a more specific theme. You might do this by using a concordance to do a word study on mountains or the sea and find out how these elements of God's world figured in certain Bible stories or how they illustrate some other teaching. Be as creative as time permits, and allow your children to share in the word search.

We have provided five devotions surrounding the topic of God's greatness. You might use opportunities of travel or outdoor fun to point out elements of God's creation. Take time to talk about the characteristics of God. Focusing on who God is can be an important factor in learning who we are in him. This week is also an excellent time to review God's plan for salvation. We hope these devotions will help spark stimulating discussions in your family.

Family Vacation

■ Devotion #1: The Creator God

This week as you focus on God's greatness, take time to consider God's creation and to thank him for being the great Creator and controller of the world. Help your children to see themselves as God's good creation as well.

Important Scripture Passages
Genesis 1–2
Psalm 139
Psalm 148
Isaiah 40:25-26; 42:5-8; 45:18-25
Ephesians 1:4-6
Colossians 1:15-20
Revelation 4:9-11

Wrapping It Up
The following devotional might be helpful in summarizing your Scripture reading of the past week, especially if your children are preschool and lower elementary-school aged.

God's Good Creation

Everywhere I go
This is what I see . . .
God's small creation
Looking up at me.

Little fragrant flowers,
Violets, bluebells.
Funny fish and birds,
Pebbles and seashells.

Everywhere I go
This is what I see . . .
God's big creation
Looking down at me.

Elephants and whales,
Trees and hills so high.
Big rocks and islands,
Clouds across the sky.

Everywhere I go
This is what I see . . .
God's great creation
In front and back of me.

Huge, towering mountains,
Waves and rolling seas.
Sparkling stars and moon,
Winds and blowing breeze.

I look in the mirror,
This is what I see . . .
God's best creation
Looking back at me!

Curly hair like Mom.
Bright eyes like my dad.
God planned and made me
To love him—I'm glad!

Questions to answer and talk about:
Can you name more of God's small creations?
Can you name more of God's big creations?
Do you think children are God's best creation? Why or
    why not?
Did God plan and make you?
What things are special about you?

Things to do:
Make a list of your favorite things in God's creation. Draw
    each one. Make a book. (You might want to illustrate
    the poem, "God's Good Creation," for your book.)

Tell each person in your family what you think is special about him or her.

———

This devotional might be helpful in summarizing your Scripture reading of the past week if your children are older elementary or junior high aged.

Who, Me?

Lindy pulled her denim jacket tight against the winter wind that blasted her when she came out the gym doors. She and Amy had yelled themselves hoarse cheering for the varsity basketball team and then jumped up screaming when the buzzer rang—their school's team had won by three points in overtime! They pushed through the crowd of students and parents to make a run for Amy's car; it was late, and they still had homework to do.

As Lindy slid past an old man in a dark overcoat, she met his eyes for just a moment. His hand reached out to touch her sleeve, and he said, "Jesus loves *you,* young lady!

Lindy dashed after Amy.

An hour later, with her trig assignment ready to hand in, Lindy snuggled down under her blankets in the dark. She remembered the soft-spoken man outside the gym. It was an interesting possibility: Did Jesus really love her—did he even *know* her?

DNA and All That Jazz

God knows Lindy all right! He's known us all since before we were born. We humans can study DNA and chromosomes and try to guess what characteristics an unborn child might have, but God knows all along. And he pays close attention, too!

165

For you created my inmost being;
*   you knit me together in my mother's womb.*
I praise you because I am fearfully and
*   wonderfully made;*
*   your works are wonderful,*
*   I know that full well.*
My frame was not hidden from you
*   when I was made in the secret place.*
When I was woven together in the depths
*   of the earth,*
*   your eyes saw my unformed body.*
All the days ordained for me
*   were written in your book*
*   before one of them came to be.*
How precious to me are your thoughts, O God!
Psalm 139:13-17

Before the World Began

Jesus has been loving Lindy and the rest of us for a long, long time, and his act of love in dying on the cross made a way for us to be right with God. God has been waiting for Lindy and for us to choose to be part of his family.

> *For he chose us in him before the creation of the world to be holy and blameless in his sight. In love he predestined us to be adopted as his sons through Jesus Christ, in accordance with his pleasure and will—to the praise of his glorious grace, which he has freely given us in the One he loves. Ephesians 1:4-6*

When did you first learn that God knew and loved you? Who told you about God's love?

Doesn't it feel great to have someone know you so completely that he knew you before you were born and chose you before the world began? Thank God for his wonderful love. Thank him for knowing you before you were born and choosing you before the world began.*

■ Devotion #2: The Powerful, Sovereign God

During this special week of extended time together as a family, focus on how BIG God is—how powerful, loving, and awesome. The following Scriptures will help you and your children praise our great God.

Important Scripture Passages

Exodus 15:1-18	Psalm 77:11-20
Deuteronomy 10:14-21	Psalm 89:5-18
Psalm 24	Psalm 93
Psalm 29	Isaiah 40:10-31
Psalm 46:10; 47; 50:1-6	Revelation 15:1-4
Psalm 71:14-24	

Wrapping It Up

The following devotional might be helpful in summarizing your Scripture reading of the past week, especially if your children are preschool and lower elementary-school aged.

Matt at Camp

Matt could hardly wait for the old bus to stop bumping and thumping up the curving dirt road. He could see Wild Woods Camp through the trees—his favorite summer camp! He had already met a friend on the bus— Scuzzy (at least that was his nickname). They were going to try to bunk in the same cabin.

Matt and Scuzzy were the first ones through the bus doors, the first ones to grab bunks next to each other,

Adapted from Annette Heinrich, One in a Zillion, Shaw, 1990.

and the first ones to the Pizza Pigout at the dining hall for supper.

When they were so full they could hardly waddle, Riff, their counselor, announced that all week they would be learning about God, the Creator, and they would begin by going on an "I Can't See, Just Smell" walk.

As soon as it was good and dark, Riff led them out onto the trail. The boys felt their way carefully through the woods with only the moonlight to show them where to walk. All the boys stopped when Riff did.

"Now smell," said Riff. "What do you smell?"

"Pine needles," they shouted. "Evergreen trees! Fresh air."

"Good," said Riff. "You can tell you're deep in the woods."

After some more stumbling along and a few turns through the trees, Riff stopped again.

"What do you smell now?" he asked.

"Water! Fish! The smoke of a campfire!" came the replies.

"So where are we?" asked Riff.

"By the lake," they all guessed.

"Right," answered Riff.

Riff cut around another way and led them back toward camp—or was it? It was just too dark to tell.

"Smell again," ordered Riff when they stopped.

"I smell . . . flowers!" shouted the boys.

"These smell sweet," said Scuzzy.

"These don't," said another boy. "They smell like my mom's cooking spices."

The boys all guessed that they were by the flower beds in front of the main meeting hall.

Before the boys went to sleep that night, they talked with Riff about how God had planned—not only beauty for their eyes, but beauty for their noses as well.

The next morning came almost too soon. After a great breakfast of scrambled eggs and bacon, Riff handed each camper a list of places around Wild Woods Camp.

"This is a Beauty for Your Eyes hunt, boys," he explained. "Follow the clues to find these places. When you do, put a check on your list. The first boys to find all the spots get a special prize at the campfire tonight!" A loud cheer went up.

Matt and Scuzzy set out together and, sure enough, they were the first ones to find Beauty Spot #1.

"Wow, Matt, look!" exclaimed Scuzzy. They were deep in a circle of trees. High above their heads the treetops arched together like a church ceiling. Only a little sunlight could get through the thick, leafy branches, so it made the air and light look all green.

"This is so beautiful," said Matt. "And it smells just like the woods last night."

The boys read the next clue, then ran as fast as they could for Spot #2. Suddenly they found themselves standing at the edge of the woods overlooking Wild Woods Lake.

The sun sparkled on the tips of the dancing waves. To the boys, it looked like a painting in blue and white with a yellow sun above. Now it was Matt's turn to say, "Wow, Scuzzy! Look at that view. God really did make beauty for our eyes!"

Then they heard voices behind them. The other boys were catching up! They quickly read the next clues and rushed to Spot #3.

"We should have guessed," groaned Matt. "It's the flower beds. We went to all the same places today that we walked to last night!"

"Yeah," agreed Scuzzy. "Only now we can use our eyes."

The boys looked down to discover flowers of every kind and color—reds and oranges and yellows and white—and everywhere around and in between was the deep green of the stems and leaves. It was very beautiful to their eyes.

That night at the campfire Matt and Scuzzy each got a pair of crazy sunglasses for being first in the Beauty for Your Eyes Hunt.

Even though he liked them, Matt wasn't thinking much about his glasses. He kept thinking about the beauty he had seen that day and about God, who had made it. He started talking to God.

"God," he said as he watched the bonfire shoot high and higher in hot, bright color. "You even made fire beautiful." Then Matt looked above the bonfire to a star-packed sky. "Wow," he said one more time. "God, you have made this whole world beautiful! You must be very, very smart and very, very strong. But God, you seem so far away—as far away as your stars. I wish you were closer. I wish you were right down here with me. Someday, God, would you be close to me?"

Nobody answered him. No words came to Matt. He heard the crickets chirp. He heard the frogs "galumf." He heard the fire spark and crack. Nothing else. Nothing more.

Matt and Scuzzy went back to their cabin to bed.

Questions to answer and talk about:
What beautiful things did Matt and Scuzzy smell?
What beautiful things did they see?
Why does Matt think God is smart?
Why does he think God is strong?

———

This devotional might be helpful in summarizing your Scripture reading of the past week if your children are older elementary or junior high aged.

Not What I Expected

The buzzer rang, and immediately the room was filled with the noise of papers being stuffed into notebooks, backpacks zipping, desk chairs scraping, and shuffling feet. Over the commotion, Rick Watkins heard Mr. Rodwell's stern voice call out, "Mr. Watkins, I want a word with you!"

Rick's best friend Max made a face at him—the grimace of doom, he called it—and disappeared out the door with the rest of the class.

Rick's stomach hurt. What had he done now? Weren't things bad enough at home—with Dad sick for so long and Mom losing her job—without him getting into more trouble at school? He moved to the front of the room and stood nervously in front of Mr. Rodwell's desk.

Dr. Jekyll and Mr. Hyde

"Richard," Mr. Rodwell began, "I'm going to a Bulls basketball game tonight, but I have an extra ticket. I thought you might like to go with me. I know your folks have been rather tied up with other things these past few weeks, and I thought you might like a chance to get out of the house."

Rick looked up at Mr. Rodwell in amazement—no fooling, the teacher was actually acting *nice* to him.

"Yeah, sure—thanks!" said Rick.

Rick had a great time with Mr. Rodwell that night. He could hardly believe that this teacher was the same guy who had the toughest grading curve in school and never put up with any nonsense in his class. Mr. Rodwell was a pretty cool guy.

Not What Rick Expected

Rick didn't expect someone with such strict rules or such an authoritative position to take time to care about him.

171

That's how a lot of people think about God. They think he is so huge and so powerful that he certainly doesn't have time to think about us puny, little people!

But the fact is that God is far more powerful and glorious than we can imagine and that he also loves us more personally and tenderly than we can imagine.

In this psalm, the writer looks at God's incredible creation, and says, "How come you still care about us?"

O LORD, our Lord,
how majestic is your name in all the earth!
You have set your glory
above the heavens.
From the lips of children and infants
you have ordained praise . . .
When I consider your heavens,
the work of your fingers,
the moon and the stars,
which you have set in place,
what is man that you are mindful of him?
the son of man that you care for him?
Psalm 8:1-2a, 3-4

Powerful Love

Have you ever looked at God's world and wondered at how amazing it is that God cares for you? Have you ever read in the Psalms or other Scriptures about God's holiness and mightiness, and wondered at how it could be that he didn't just zap you off the face of the earth?

God could just zap us off the face of the earth, but because he loves us so much, he uses his power to care for us and to help us live for his kingdom.

The LORD is the everlasting God,
the Creator of the ends of the earth.
He will not grow tired or weary,
and his understanding no one can fathom.

*He gives strength to the weary
and increases the power of the weak.
Even youths grow tired and weary,
and young men stumble and fall;
but those who hope in the LORD
will renew their strength.
They will soar on wings like eagles;
they will run and not grow weary,
they will walk and not be faint.
Isaiah 40:28b-31*

Thank God now for the mystery of his greatness and power and of his tender, personal love.

**You have dared to believe God
for your own salvation. Will you believe
Him for the salvation of your children?**
CHARLES ANDERSON

■ Devotion #3: Jesus, the Savior

Through all of the history of God's dealing with people, we have never seen his greatness more than when, in his great mercy, he sent his beloved, perfect, only Son to die for us. Take time this week to explain the gift of Jesus' life, death, and resurrection. Help your children clearly understand God's plan for reconciling people to himself.

Important Scripture Passages
Matthew 1:18-23
Mark 12:28-34
John 3:16-18; 10:7-18
Romans 3:22-24
Romans 5:5-11
Romans 6:23
Ephesians 2:8-9
Titus 3:3-7
1 John 1:5-9, 2:2; 4:13-16

Wrapping It Up
The following devotional might be helpful in summarizing your Scripture reading of the past week, especially
if your children are preschool and lower elementary-
school aged.

Matt in the Dark

"Mark 12:30. Mark 12:30. Mark 12:30." Matt said the
reference over and over in his head. The only brain work
he and Scuzzy had to do that day was to learn this one
Bible verse. As soon as they could say it to Riff, their
counselor at Wild Woods Camp, they were free to join
the Outdoor Olympics going on by the beach and recrea-
tion area. It would be the greatest—high jumps and
broad jumps and running races, archery shoots, and
shotput throws!

"How are you doing, Scuzzy?" Matt asked his friend.

"O.K. I've got it all learned but the last line,"
answered Scuzzy. They both worked a few more
minutes. "I'm ready to say mine to you, Matt. Will you
listen?" Scuzzy asked. "Mark 12:30," he began. "And you
shall love the Lord your God with all your heart, and
with all your soul, and with all your mind, and with all
your strength" (RSV).

"Great! Now I'll try it," said Matt. He repeated it word
for word!

"Let's find Riff," they shouted together. They ran to
prove they finally knew their verse. Never had the boys
had such a great time as they had that day at the
Outdoor Olympics.

But something strange was happening to Matt. There
he was—at the footrace, on his mark, ready to run like
a rabbit when the starting gun fired. But the Bible verse
he had learned kept buzzing through his brain: "You
shall love the Lord your God with all your heart. You

shall love the Lord your God with all your mind." Matt tried to think about the race, but all he could think about was the verse.

When the gun fired, he ran. "You shall love the Lord your God with all your strength," he heard as the verse repeated in his mind. Matt shook his head as he sped along the track.

Then Matt's chest hit the tape across the finish line, and he knew he'd won! He also came in first in the broad jump that afternoon. Scuzzy was the best archer in the bow-and-arrow shoot. Each boy cheered the other on, then slapped his back when he won. It was great to have a friend! It was great to win a race.

But through all the games and through all the day, Matt's verse played in his mind again and again.

"Scuzzy, I think someone turned a tape on in my brain," he joked. But the verse didn't go away.

He heard it during the Big Pig Barbecue, and he heard it during campfire. He heard it while he showered, and now, here in the dark in his bunk, he heard it loudest and clearest of all.

"And you shall love the Lord your God with all your heart, and with all your soul, and with all your mind, and with all your strength."

"Wait a minute!" Matt sat straight up in his bunk. "I know what love is," he said. "I know what it feels like to love Mom and Dad, and I really love Grandma and Grandpa, too! I love baby Michael so much, and now I love my new friend, Scuzzy. But I don't feel love for God that way. I don't even *know* God, so how *can* I love him?"

He began to talk to God again. "God, it's me, Matt. I just figured out that I don't know you. Is that why you seem so far away from me? Riff says I'm a sinner—that everybody is. He's right. I've told lies and disobeyed my Dad. Jesus, will you wash away my sins and be my God?

Will you come live inside me and be close to me forever? I want to love you like the verse says."

Matt lay back down. Nobody answered him. No words came to Matt. But suddenly he felt like a Kool-Aid pitcher being filled up from the bottom to the top. He felt quiet inside—but happy, too!

"It must be Jesus coming in." Matt smiled in the dark. "It must be Jesus."

Questions to answer and talk about:
Who do you think "turned a tape on" in Matt's brain?
Which people do you love?
Who can wash away our sins?
When Jesus comes in to our hearts and lives, does he ever leave?
Can you say Matt's and Scuzzy's verse?

———

This devotional might be helpful in summarizing your Scripture reading of the past week if your children are older elementary or junior high aged.

Here Comes the Sun

Rob reached out from under his covers and tried to grab the end of the shade on the window across from his bed. He leaned a little further, and *wham!* Rob fell out of bed onto the pile of books and dirty clothes he had dumped on the floor the night before.

He grabbed the white windowshade and gave it a quick tug. *Zoom—smack, thwack!* It flew up to the top and flopped around the cylinder twice.

Rob sat back and let the morning sun pour all over him. It was early for him to be awake on a Saturday, but he felt excited and content all at once. The feeling was so strange he just couldn't sleep it away with a pillow over his head.

He'd attended his third Bible study in a row the night before. The youth leader had explained how people were separated from God by sin and needed a way back to God. Suddenly, it felt like someone had switched a light on in Rob's head: Jesus died to make things right between him and God!

After the group time, Rob talked to the youth leader, and they prayed together. Rob had invited the God who made the whole world into his life by accepting the sacrifice of his Son, Jesus Christ.

I feel new! thought Rob, as he sat in the flood of sunlight. *This is the greatest!*

Let the Sun Shine In

A writer once said, "I believe in Christianity as I believe the sun has risen, not only because I see it but because by it I see everything else" (C.S. Lewis).

When did the lights turn on in your head about the good news of Christ? How did you feel?

> *For we do not preach ourselves, but Jesus Christ as Lord, and ourselves as your servants for Jesus' sake. For God, who said, "Let light shine out of darkness," made his light shine in our hearts to give us the light of the knowledge of the glory of God in the face of Christ. 2 Corinthians 4:5-6*

Life through 3-D Glasses

Suddenly life seemed different to Rob. Accepting Christ was like putting on 3-D glasses: it changed the colors and dimensions of everything—home and his family, school and his friends, and life in the world.

When you gave your life to God, what seemed different to you? Do you see a difference in the way you look at the world and the way your friends who don't know Jesus look at the world?

Thank God for the gift of life in Christ. Thank him for a new way of seeing.*

■ Devotion #4: The Holy Spirit

It's sometimes difficult for children or young people to realize that the Holy Spirit is with them—after all, we can't see his physical presence. But your children can know that they have God's great gift of himself with them at all times, and that he is the ultimate power source for living.

Important Scripture Passages

Isaiah 44:3-4	2 Corinthians 1:21-22;
Luke 11:9-13	3:17-18
John 14:25-27	Galatians 5:16-25
Acts 1:1-11	Ephesians 1:13-14;
Romans 8:5-16, 26-27	2:19-22; 3:16-21; 5:18-20
1 Corinthians 6:19-20	1 John 3:23-24; 4:13-16

Wrapping It Up

The following devotional might be helpful in summarizing your Scripture reading of the past week, especially if your children are preschool and lower elementary-school aged.

Matt Upside Down

The Bike Race Biggie was about to begin. It was the final fun event at Wild Woods Camp before the bus pulled out for home. Matt and Scuzzy tried not to be sad at leaving each other. They had promised to call and write letters.

*Adapted from Annette Heinrich, One in a Zillion, Shaw, 1990.

Right now they weren't thinking about the bus, though. What they were thinking about was the bike race and how to win. They checked to make sure their water bottles were full and their seats at the right height.

Riff, their counselor, shouted out the rules. "Stay on the main path! No shortcuts allowed! Don't ride too close beside other bikes, and may the best man win!"

With a raucous cheer and a powerful puff of dust, the bikers were off. They pedaled as fast as they could, pushing and pumping with all their might. Matt noticed that every now and then his chain slipped--and he also noticed that every other boy except one had pulled ahead of him. Now that boy was gaining on him, too. He changed gears and pedaled faster, but the boy sped past him.

Suddenly Matt saw a shortcut through the woods. No one would see him go that way, since he was the last rider. If he took the cutoff, he could get out in front of the other boys by a good bit. He might even win the race!

He started to turn his handlebars toward the side path when Riff's words came back to him: "No shortcuts! Stay on the path!"

Matt began to talk to God. "Thank you for reminding me, God. Please help me to obey the rules." Matt pulled his bike sharply back to the main path and began to pump hard on the pedals.

Thud! Matt's front tire hit something on the path! *How could I miss seeing such a big rock?* he wondered as he flipped up in the air. He sailed over the handlebars, landed hard on the ground, then rolled upside-down against a big sugar pine beside the path. Poor Matt! He hurt. His head and shoulder hurt; his ankle hurt. And he felt mad because he knew he had lost the race.

After a few minutes, he tried to get up. But when he put his foot down, his leg bent under and he fell back against the tree.

I'm in big trouble, thought Matt. It was beginning to be a habit, so he started talking to God again. "God," he said, "this is your friend Matt. I need your help. Thanks for helping me obey the rules. But now I'm hurt and no one knows because I was last in line. Please send someone to help!"

Nobody answered him. No words came to Matt. But what *did* he hear? A sound like the whirr of bike tires— and the sound of Riff's whistle when he was happy.

"Riff!" shouted Matt. "Hey, Riff!"

Riff jumped from his bike and knelt beside Matt. "Don't worry, Matt. I'll be back with the camp doctor and a stretcher in no time," he said, and away he went.

"Thank you, God," prayed Matt. "You sure sent help in a hurry."

While Matt waited for Riff he sang, "Thank you, Lord, for saving my soul. Thank you, Lord, for making me whole. Thank you, Lord, for giving to me, Your great salvation so rich and free!"

And while he sang, his mad feelings just melted away. Instead he felt glad all over inside. He began to pray one more time. "I've noticed something, God. First you helped me obey the rules. Then you brought me help when I needed it. Now I'm not feeling bad about losing the race anymore. You cheered me up. Thank you, Lord Jesus. I'm sure glad you gave me your Holy Spirit to live inside me. Thank you for all your help!"

Questions to answer and talk about:

The Holy Spirit is God's Spirit living in us. When did the Holy Spirit begin to live in Matt? (Parents, remind your children of the last story, "Matt in the Dark.")

What three things did God the Holy Spirit help Matt with?

Will he help us with the same kinds of problems?
Can he help us with any kind of problem?

———

This devotional might be helpful in summarizing your
Scripture reading of the past week if your children are
older elementary or junior high aged.

Power Source

Shari lay face down on her bed, crying hot tears that left
a damp streak on her blue comforter. She took her journal
out of the drawer in the nightstand, and looked up the
entry from her birthday—less than a week earlier.

"Today I turn seventeen, and I know it's time to make
some resolutions about how I treat my family. Starting
today, I'm going to be patient with Harvey, and I'm not
going to lose my temper and yell at Mom. I want them
to know I'm a Christian for real. I know I can do it!"

Ha! she thought now, *I can't even do it for a week!*
She'd been right in the middle of an important phone
conversation with her best friend Paula when she realized that someone was on the other extension of the
phone: Harvey. So she stomped off to throttle her little
brother, and Mom came in and blamed her for the whole
thing, and the next thing Shari knew she was yelling
and crying.

If at First You Don't Succeed . . .

This wasn't the first time Shari had determined to live
for Christ in her family. She'd tried it many times, and
she just couldn't make her tongue and her temper keep
her resolutions. But she kept trying. "If at first you don't
succeed, try, try again" was her motto.

I've got news for Shari: it's not going to work. Sure,
she needs to work hard at controlling her temper and

guarding her sharp tongue. And her hard work will help—a little. But there's a much better way for Shari to tackle the temper-and-tongue project.

God's motto is different from Shari's. His says, "If at first you don't succeed, realize you need my help!"

What Could Be Better than Jesus?

Before his death and resurrection, Jesus told his disciples, "It's good for you that I'm going away—because someone even better will come after me!" I'm sure his disciples were confused. Thy probably asked each other, "Who could be better than Jesus?"

> But I tell you the truth: It is for your good that I am going away. Unless I go away, the Counselor will not come to you; but if I go, I will send him to you. John 16:7

The Holy Spirit is the "Counselor" Jesus talked about. And the Holy Spirit that lives in you is your ever-ready power source for living your life for Christ.

What areas of sin do you struggle with in the way Shari struggles with keeping her temper? Have you ever made resolutions to "do better"? How did it work out? Have you ever asked the Lord for the Holy Spirit's power to help you in that situation?

Talk to God again right now about your problem areas. Thank him for the best gift, his Spirit.

> I pray that out of his glorious riches he may strengthen you with power through his Spirit in your inner being, so that Christ may dwell in your hearts through faith. And I pray that you, being rooted and established in love, may have power, together with all the saints, to grasp how wide and long and high and deep is the love of Christ, and to know this love that

surpasses knowledge—that you may be filled
to the measure of all the fullness of God.
Ephesians 3:16-21*

■ Devotion #5: The Everlasting God

As you and your children focus on God's greatness, who he is and what he has done for us, be sure to remind your family that God is our God forever. God is faithful to fulfill all his promises to his people—forever! If your children are older, you might do a Scripture word-search using the words "everlasting," "eternal," and "forever" to discover Scriptures that praise the God who reigns forever. Some are provided for you below.

Important Scripture Passages

Psalm 9:7-10	Psalm 145
Psalm 48	Isaiah 26:3-4
Psalm 90:1-2	Hebrews 1:8; 13:8
Psalm 103:17-19	1 John 5:20
Psalm 111	Revelation 1:17-18
Psalm 136	

Wrapping It Up

The following devotional might be helpful in summarizing your Scripture reading of the past week, especially if your children are preschool and lower elementary-school aged.

How Far Is Forever?

Mandi's family was reading the Bible together.

"The Lord lives on forever," her brother read (Psalm 9:7, TLB).

"He is the true God and eternal life," was Mama's part (1 John 5:20, NIV).

---

*Adapted from Annette Heinrich, Not a Hollywood Family, Shaw, 1989.

"From everlasting to everlasting, you are God," read Papa (Psalm 90:2, NIV).

"So our God will live forever," explained Papa, "because he is eternal. He is an everlasting God."

"But how far is forever?" Mandi wanted to know.

"Farther than your eyes can see," they all said.

"Farther than I can see from the upstairs window?" Mandi asked.

"Let's go see," said Brother. They went upstairs together to her bedroom. He held her up to the window in his strong arms so she could see across the treetops and shingled roofs all the way to the city. "Yes, Mandi," Brother said, "forever is farther than we can see from this window!"

"Is it farther than I can see from a city skyscraper?" Mandi asked Mama.

"Let's go see," said Mama. They rode up in the elevator to the very top of the tallest building in the whole city. Mandi peered over the tops of towers and skyscrapers far away to the mountains. "Yes, Mandi," said Mama, "forever is farther than we can see from this skyscraper."

"Is it farther than we can see from the mountains?" Mandi asked Papa.

"Let's go see," said Papa. They drove up and up to the highest peak of the highest mountain. There they stood with the wind whistling past and looked far, far away across the valleys and the hills and the city and the towns. "Yes, Mandi," said Papa, "forever is farther than our eyes can see even from the mountaintop."

"Forever is very far," said Mandi.

"How much is eternal?" Mandi wanted to know.

"More than your arms can hold," they all said.

"Yes," said Mandi, "but is eternal more than my pool can hold?"

"Let's go see," said Brother. He held her hand as they walked to the back yard. They circled the pool. "Yes, Mandi," said Brother, "eternal is more than your pool can hold."

"Is it more than our lake can hold?" Mandi asked Mama.

"Let's go see," said Mama. They walked around the quiet lake together, then stepped out onto the dock. They looked past the islands across to the other shore. "Yes, Mandi," said Mama, "eternal is more than our lake can hold."

"But is eternal more than the ocean can hold?" Mandi asked Papa.

"Let's go see," he said. They stood high on a rock by the seashore with the salt water spraying their faces and looked far, far away across the waves to the edge of the world. "Yes, Mandi," Papa said, "eternal is more than even the ocean can hold."

"Eternal is very much!" said Mandi.

"How long is everlasting?" Mandi wanted to know.

"As long as many tomorrows," her family said.

"Is everlasting longer than from now until my birthday?" Mandi asked her brother.

"Let's go see," he answered. Brother turned the calendar to Mandi's birthday. He put a red "X" on her special day. "Yes, Mandi," he said, "everlasting is longer than from now until your birthday."

"But is it longer than from now until Christmas?" Mandi asked Mama.

"Let's go see," said Mama. She turned more calendar pages until it said, "December." She put a green circle around Christmas Day. "Yes, Mandi," said Mama. "Everlasting is longer than from now until Christmas.'

"Then how long *is* everlasting?" Mandi asked Papa.

Papa lifted Mandi to his lap and hugged her close. "Everlasting is a sun that never has a sunset," Papa said. "Everlasting is a song that never stops singing. Everlasting is a story that never says, 'The End.'"

"Everlasting is very long," said Mandi. And she kissed her Papa goodnight.

Questions to answer and talk about:

I will tell you a secret about Mandi's three words: forever, eternal, and everlasting. They all mean the same thing! If forever and eternal and everlasting were a long string, do you think it would have an end?

Does God's life ever end?

Does our life ever end when the Holy Spirit lives in us?

What happens to us when we die?

————

This devotional might be helpful in summarizing your Scripture reading of the past week if your children are older elementary or junior high aged.

Good-byes

As the station wagon turned the corner of their road for the last time, Megan looked back to see her best friend Carla waving as hard as she could. It didn't make her feel better, though. Mama saw her crying, and passed her the box of Kleenex.

Megan felt as if she couldn't take one more good-bye! Her grandfather had died four months before, and that had been hard. Losing Grandpa was the first time Megan had to say good-bye to someone that she loved. Then her father's company had promoted him—and that meant a transfer to another state. The family's moving plans didn't include "Sandy," their horse. Sandy wouldn't fit into the suburban neighborhood where

Megan's family was going. So Megan had to say good-bye to Sandy, too. Now she was leaving behind Carla, who said she would write every week, but Megan wondered how long that would last.

"Why does everything have to change?" she cried.

Changes
Good-byes are one of the hardest parts about living and loving here on earth. It does seem that situations and relationships are continually changing, and it's often hard to find a solid place for your feelings to rest.

Have you ever been disappointed because a relationship has changed? Have you ever wished that things wouldn't change? Have you seen changes in your own family this past year? Have you seen changes in yourself?

From Everlasting to Everlasting
The only person who never changes is God. He never goes away, he never stops loving, he always keeps his promises, and he is always faithful to his people. God was there before the world began, and God will be there forever and ever.

> *"I am the Alpha and the Omega, the Beginning and the End. To him who is thirsty I will give to drink without cost from the spring of the water of life. He who overcomes will inherit all this, and I will be his God and he will be my son." Revelation 21:6-7*

> *Lord, you have been our dwelling place*
> *throughout all generations.*
> *Before the mountains were born*
> *or you brought forth the earth and*
> *the world,*
> *from everlasting to everlasting you are God.*
> *Psalm 90:1-2*

When everything around you is changing, hang on to the Lord. He can be your "dwelling place," a place of unchanging love and security. You can rest in God because his love never ends.

Just for Fun

If you've squeezed lots of fun activities into your summer schedule, yet still have room for more, here are a few additional summer-fun possibilities for you and your family.

How Does Your Garden Grow?

We've already talked about working in the yard as a family, but gardening is a creative step beyond general upkeep like mowing and raking. Our family hasn't experienced all that much success in vegetable gardening—even if Dad did grow up on a farm. The times we've tried it, the elements and the rabbits have conspired against us! Everyone teases Mom (Joyce) about how she served green beans for supper one night, including a solitary green bean from our garden's produce. If that garden only produced one green bean, Mom was determined to feed it to the family! But Mom was and is a masterful flower gardener, and we all took turns helping her plant and weed and water.

Your children may especially enjoy their share in the garden if they are involved in plotting the garden and in choosing the vegetables or flowers you will plant there. My husband David recommends allowing each child a small plot all his own. As a boy, he grew puny, somewhat inedible muskmelons in his back yard. Now he grows orchids, and I admit I'm grateful for the change! Even if your child has his own plot, he will still require a great deal of supervision from Mom or Dad.

Gardening is an enormously satisfying pastime because it pays in dividends of great beauty or of useful contribution to the family food stores. A fistful of cool, damp, brown dirt can be even more fun than play dough!

Some smaller gardening efforts can be started indoors and later moved outside. Here are a few such projects.

Plant a sunflower seed. Hardly anything grows so fast and dramatically tall as the sunflower. It is exciting for younger children to see the first shoots sprout from the seeds they planted in a cup just days before. When the flower is a few inches tall, transplant it to a sunny spot. When the sunflower is at full height, photograph your child in front of it.

Plant grass seed in soil in a plastic cup. Draw a funny face on the cup so when the grass sprouts, the funny face will have green "hair." When the "hair" gets long, give him a haircut! Then transplant to a needy spot in your lawn.

Start a sweet potato vine (this one should remain indoors). Poke round toothpicks into the base of a sweet potato about two or three inches from the bottom. Fill a clear glass or pint jar with water and suspend the potato on the glass with the tip in the water. If you keep the water level constant, before long, roots will grow downward and a beautiful green vine will grow up. Tie one or two long pieces of string from the glass to the ceiling, and the vine will eventually twist and train all the way up!

Feed the Birds

Construct a birdfeeder in a place that is visible from the house. Although your neighborhood bird friends may not need much of your help in the summertime months, your summer work of building the birdfeeder will bring both you and some hungry feathered friends much pleasure this winter.

If you have woodworking talent in the family, look at some sample feeders and do it yourself. But feel free to seek out the easily put-together kits available at hardware stores, or buy a feeder that is ready to hang.

You might want to invest in a book about birds. By the time he was twelve, my brother Marc was a young ornithologist. He studied our bird books and borrowed Dad's binoculars to go bird watching. He could tell us all when we'd spotted a yellow-bellied sapsucker, a ruby-throated hummingbird, or a red-winged blackbird. Have a resource ready for naming the types of birds that live in your area.

Puppet Play

Puppet-making and puppet shows make wonderful summertime fun! You might use socks or lunchsacks to make simple hand puppets. Your children may already own several hand puppets. When we children were small, Mom used a large, upright moving box to make us a small puppet theater. She covered the box with bright contact paper, cut a square, TV-size hole in the top of one side, and sewed a bright curtain to hang across the hole. One or two children could enter the box from behind, kneel under the "stage" opening, and operate the puppets for the family's entertainment.

Shadow puppets are another creative type of puppet play. Children can easily construct shadow puppet shapes simply by drawing them on sturdy paper and cutting out the pieces. These pieces are then attached to a straw or a chopstick or some other extending piece. These puppets are not actually seen by the audience, but their shadows cast on the wall will tell the story.

A shadow puppet theater is created by finding a pale, blank wall (or by hanging a sheet on a wall) and then posting a lamp a short distance in front of it. You may want to set up a shield for the puppeteers by blocking the lamp area with two chairs and a blanket.

Puppet play is excellent creative exercise for little people. Their storytelling and handcraft and performance skills will benefit from a few hours of puppet show production.

Baking

We've touched on kitchen duty earlier in this book, but I want to express again the importance of letting your children "invade your space" during cooking and baking hours. I (Annette) honestly thought I knew next to nothing about cooking when I got married, but I found that I had many memories of "the way Mom used to do it." But I did know how to bake, and my lessons came from baking with Mom.

Your baking will take twice as long when your child helps and may create ten times the disaster in your kitchen, but both you and your child should come away with a warm feeling of satisfaction. You'll feel satisfied because you spent quality time in a fun and educational activity with your child. Your child will feel proud of the baked goods you have produced together, and will be happy about the time you concentrated solely on him.

Or turn the kitchen over to an older child for a create-your-own-recipe attempt. If the project turns out great, write down the recipe and add it to your file for a repeat performance. Our friend Betty's son created peanut-butter ball cookies on his first try, and my brother Marc reproduced the cool, refreshing taste of an Orange Julius.

There will be disasters, of course. I was ten or eleven the first time Mom let me try chocolate-chip cookies by myself—my brother said they were harder than rocks and asked if we could line the driveway with them! But I remember how proud I was to bring my father the small chocolate cake I had made for his birthday—even though Mom had baked a big one. Dad was so pleased with my work for him. A success like that goes a long way for a little girl!

Your Very Own Restaurant
Together with your children, brainstorm decor, food, and entertainment ideas for an evening with special friends or relatives. Turn your living room into an Italian or French restaurant, with your children creating menus, helping prepare food, acting as hosts, hostesses, waiters, and waitresses, and clean-up crew, and providing entertainment. Invite Grandpa or Grandma on an anniversary, or invite another family with whom you enjoy spending time. Your children will enjoy the grown-up role-playing of an adult occupation, and the activity provides an enjoyable context for serving others.

Provide younger children with a large box or a board set on bricks for an outdoor restaurant. Make a sign proclaiming "McPlacas" or "McHeinrichs" (or whatever your name is) and let your children create mudpie hamburgers, puddle cold drinks, grass & weed salads, wet sand cookies, etc. The children can make their own play money for their friends to spend. Paper plates, cups, and napkins will add to the fun (and will help in cleanup).

Pajama Raid
While his children were young, my pastor had a spontaneous summertime tradition. After all children were safely tucked in, prayed with, and kissed good-night, they'd hear a call from downstairs: "Pajama Raid!" Mom and Dad would pile their pajama'd children into the car and head for Dairy Queen. The giggles and delight were well worth the chocolate smears down nightgown fronts and p.j. shirts. Those children enjoy that memory of their parents as spontaneous and fun-loving.

Bubble Fun

Summer fun wouldn't be complete without blowing bubbles! Pack a bottle of commercial bubbles along for each child when you go to the park for a picnic. Or make a pan of your own "Bubble Batter" for instant fun in the backyard. Here are two favorite recipes to try:

Bubble Batter #1
1 cup water
½ cup sudsy detergent
1 Tbs sugar

Bubble Batter #2
2 cups water
½ cup liquid detergent
2 Tbs vegetable oil

Commercial bubble wands and pipes can be purchased at toy centers. With some creative effort, you and your children can produce giant bubbles. Scoop through the bubble batter with large and small cans with both ends removed. Or see what you can produce with a wire coat hanger shaped in a circle. Here's a good recipe for the really big bubbles (use a large pail for mixing):

Giant Bubble Batter
1 cup dish detergent (Joy or Dawn is best)
3-4 Tbs glycerine (from a drug store)
10-15 cups clean, cold water
Stir gently

Your children might enjoy bubble painting, too. Fill a plastic cup 3/4 full with a combination of water, detergent, and food coloring. Outdoors, set the cup on a sheet of paper, insert a straw, and blow and blow until you have bubbled colored suds onto your painting. Combine colors on your artwork by using several cups, each containing a different color.

Quiet Time

Our friend Margie recommends short "peace-and-quiet-reading times" after lunch during summer weekdays.

During days primarily consumed with rough-and-tumble pastimes, she felt it was important for her kids to take a breather. This reading time reinforces the cognitive skills that are exercised less frequently during non-school months.

This reading time could be an hour of rest for you, too. Or perhaps it could be another opportunity to spend one-on-one time with your children. Mom could rotate with the days—Sarah's turn on Monday, Peter on Tuesday, Mom's day off on Wednesday, Sarah again on Thursday, etc. My friend Alice spent long, patient hours listening to her son, Joel, practice his reading skills. He found reading difficult, especially in the more tense and competitive atmosphere at school. Those safe, quiet hours with Mom made a difference in his reading ability.

Parade
Your town will probably have some sort of parade during the summer months. Summertime holds Memorial Day, the Fourth of July, and Labor Day—and your town may have other festival days in between. Even though it is a major hassle for you to pack up lawn chairs or blankets, popcorn, flags, and children, make the effort to attend at least one of these summer parades. You may be surprised that such a passive event as watching bands and floats go by can be transformed into the action-packed adventure your kids will make it. Very likely they'll run all over, seeing friends or clowns or big horses or fire trucks. No doubt you'll all come home full of sun and fun, and ready for a bath and bed.

Take Me Out to the Ballgame
Sporting events can be major-league excitement for little people—from the big leagues down to the church's softball playoffs. Many children collect paraphernalia of local sports heroes, and a trip to a sporting event featuring one of these celebrities is a lifelong memory-maker.

One large family we know leaves their little ones home with a sitter on days when they head out to sporting events. This way, their attention is freed up for their older children during an event with little appeal for very young children.

Music

I'll admit that Mom and Dad dragged us—despite tremendous protests—to the local philharmonic each month. But, believe it or not, though we active young bodies disliked being cooped up on the very last row of the balcony (the cheapest seats) for two hours, we all grew up to enjoy classical music.

Many communities have special musical presentations that are offered free in city parks or band shelters during spring and summer months. These could be enjoyable occasions for getting out in the evening cool with neighbors and friends. There are other areas of the country that have regular outdoor-theater professional symphonies. Bring along a picnic, and enjoy the bright sounds under a summer sky.

Take a Walk

An old song sings the virtues of having a "heart-to-heart" talk while taking "an old-fashioned walk." Almost anytime is good for a walk—and almost anyplace! We'd like to suggest some themes and purposes for walks. Some are for experiencing the beauties of God's creations; some are for gaining useful information about that creation.

Sunrise Walk. Walk where you'll have the best view of the eastern sky and enjoy a sunrise.

Full Moon Walk. Walk by the light of the moon. Enjoy how different familiar places look and sound at night. Find the constellations you usually see in books.

Wet and Rainy Walk. Choose a warm day with gentle rain—and no lightning, of course! Enjoy the sound and feel of the raindrops on and around you, and smell the pungent aroma of rain-soaked earth. Take time for some puddle-stomping.

Tree Walk. Search for different kinds of trees. Compare evergreen and deciduous; compare maple and birch bark; compare evergreen needles and other leaves. Collect some samples for sorting and naming later. Talk about how the tree "plants" its seeds. Investigate whether the tree bears fruit or nuts.

Bird Walk. Look for common birds of your area. Bring along a pocket bird book for help. Make a list of birds you see. Wait quietly to catch bird calls and songs. Try to spot a bird's nest. When you get home, learn to appreciate nest-building skills by trying to recreate a nest yourself, using only the items a bird uses.

Insect Walk. Investigate for insects. Perhaps begin a bug collection.

Circle and Shape Walk. See how many circles you can find in nature (dandelion and other flower faces, tree stump surfaces, clover heads, the sun, leaves, etc.). Do you discover any squares, rectangles, or triangles?

Texture Walk. Walk barefoot in your yard or a park. Talk about various textures your feet detect—rough, smooth, slippery, bumpy, gritty. What things have which textures?

Summer Sounds Walk. Listen as you walk for sounds that are heard distinctly in summer—crickets, frogs, mosquitoes, cicadas, birds, rain, thunder. List the ones you identify.

Nature Walk. Carry along a bottle of glue, and provide each child with a paper plate. As they find pods, pine cones, evergreen needles, clover leaves, etc., let the children glue them to the plate in a nature collage.

Trash Bag Walk. Take grocery bags or trash bags to an area near your home that attracts litter. Do your part to beautify God's world by picking up the mess.

Be creative! You'll think of other kinds of walks. Take along binoculars. Young children might want to make their own "binoculars" by gluing two empty toilet-paper rolls together and stapling a yarn cord to the top. These might be decorated with markers.

Also take along a favorite trail mix. Our favorite is to mix plain popcorn, cheese popcorn, M & Ms, raisins, sunflower seeds (and anything else you enjoy) together. Portion into individual bags for each hiker.

Take a Ride

To a Secret Place. Let your child call a best friend. Let them pack lunches and ride their bicycles to a secret spot for lunch (doesn't every child have a secret place?).

On a Horse. If funds permit, visit a riding stable for a ride on a real horse. Or search out pony rides in your area, perhaps at a local festival or fair.

On a Haywagon. Have a summer hayride, and invite other friends or cousins. A moonlight ride can be a special adventure.

On a Bus. Many children raised in the country or suburbs seldom ride a city bus.

On a Train. Many cities have special times and places to board the train and ride from one spot and back again in just a few hours.

Host the Neighborhood

For a Children's Garage Sale. Invite neighbor children to mark the toys they'd like to exchange for cash and bring them to your driveway for a four- or five-hour garage sale. Be sure to put out signs—and make lots of Kool-Aid for the kids. If children want to bake ahead of time, this could be a toy-and-bake sale.

For a Bike Wash. On a hot day, set out rags, soapy water, and a hose for rinsing down the bikes once they're scrubbed. Provide full-sized old towels for drying and polishing. Suggest bathing suits or old shorts and shirts for this kind of work. And let your Bike Wash precede a Bike Parade.

For a Bike Parade. Allow your children to prepare flyers and posters to announce the date, time, and place to assemble. Dad or Mom will help by reproducing flyers on a copier. Each parade entry must be decorated. The parade should include children of all ages, so welcome trikes, bikes, and wagons. The parade route should pass all the homes of the children riding and might end up at your house for popsicles or ice cream cones.

For a Stuffed Pet Competition. Invite neighborhood children to come with their favorite stuffed animals. Provide grocery boxes, open on one side, for cages. The boxes can be decorated with markers. Let each child choose a spot on the lawn to display his caged pet. Ask big brothers or sisters to act as judges. Homemade ribbons (made from stickers and sasheen ribbon) will be awarded to each pet. (Choose pink, orange, or yellow ribbon to avoid the blue, red, and white colors of actual first, second, third prizes.) Follow the show with refreshments of animal crackers and milk.

Color Collision

Sidewalk Art. Provide colored chalk for the children to draw pictures on the sidewalks or driveway. Rain will take care of the clean-up.

Ice Cube Paint. Freeze a popsicle stick into ice cube trays or popsicle forms filled with water. When they're hard, sprinkle dry tempera on paper, then use the ice cube as a brush.

Rock Painting. Collect rocks as big as your hand. Have the children wash them and put them in the sun to dry. Children will love to paint the rocks bright colors for use as paperweights, door stops, or a colorful border for flowerbeds.

Colored Necklaces. String Fruit Loops onto yarn for a colorful and edible necklace. A piece of tape on one end holds it firm for threading; a fruit loop tied to the other end keeps the other loops from falling off.

Lunch-Sack Art. Use crayons or markers to cover a lunch bag with colored art. Each artist can pack his bag with a sandwich he made himself, fruit, and cookies. Picnic at a favorite spot!

Green Eggs and Ham. Before lunch, read the story *Green Eggs & Ham* (see *Suggested Reading for Kids*). Then prepare green eggs by adding green food coloring to scrambled eggs.

Color Real Flowers. Teach absorption by cutting fresh white flowers from your garden. Place their stems in glasses containing water with red or blue food coloring. As the flowers "drink" the water, the petal edges will turn red or blue. Carnations work especially well.

Color Equations. Using clear glasses of water, add combinations of food coloring drops. For example, red and blue in one glass, red and yellow in another, and blue and yellow in another. Write a color equation for each glass, such as: Red + Blue = Purple. For pre-readers, make the equations with crayon stripes of the colors instead of using words.

Butterfly Blots. Put two blobs of colored tempera, one above the other, on a plain sheet of paper. Make the top blob a bit larger than the bottom one. Fold the paper in half and press together. Open to behold your butterfly blot.

Giant Butterflies. Using single sheets of colored tissue paper, gather each sheet in the middle and tie with a piece of colored yarn. For a bright splash of color on the patio or in the playroom, hang them from the ceiling or the trees.

Filter Flowers. Glue coffee filters to a large piece of construction paper. Then glue cupcake liners in the middle of the coffee filters. Color the flowers with markers and add stems and leaves by using green marker or green pipe cleaners.

Tulip Handprints. Put your hand in tulip-colored tempera (pink, red, white, yellow). Keeping your fingers together, press your hand on a paper. Add a stem to your tulip. Make a whole garden of tulips!

Face Painting. Poke through drawers to collect "almost used up" or out-of-date makeup. Provide mirrors for your children, and let them paint their own and each other's faces.

Natural Dyes. Create your own coloring or dyes by boiling berries, bark, radishes, and onion skins. What colors do they make? Will they paint? What other things might make dye?

Squirt-a-Sheet. Hang an old white sheet on the clothesline outside. Fill squirt or spray bottles (plastic only) with cold, colored water. Create a rainbow, a tie-dye look, or other patterns on the sheet. Wear a swimsuit or old clothes!

Veggie Paints. Place different tempera colors on styrofoam trays. Make pictures by using half-vegetables for printing. Dip the cut half of the veggie into the paint, then press it on paper. Use carrots, potatoes, zucchini and other squash, broccoli tips, celery leaves, corn cobs, and radishes.

No-Color Painting. For younger children, nothing is more fun than painting the side of the garage or a fence or trees, using real paintbrushes and buckets of water. The wood darkens as it gets wet, giving an illusion of paint.

So-So Sewing

On Styrofoam Trays. Using darning needles and lightweight yarn, children can learn sewing basics by punching through styrofoam meat trays that you have washed and saved.

Buttons and Scraps. Boys and girls who already know how to push a needle back and forth can learn to sew on buttons. Choose large buttons and pretty fabric scraps for practice. Include instruction on threading needles and tying knots.

Homemade Beanbags. These can be made by hand, but introductory lessons on the sewing machine (with lots of supervision) can be exciting. Cut two squares from colorful fabric scraps (each about six inches). Sew three sides together, wrong side out. Turn the bag right side out, stuff about three-quarters full with dried beans or peas. Sew down the fourth side. Play catch, make a target, or play beanbag basketball. Make up your own game, complete with rules.

Doll Clothes. Provide fabric scraps, ribbons and trims, needles and threads; gather some dolls; and see what styles your children come up with!

Build Your Own . . .

Wood Sculpture. Using wood scraps and pieces from around your home or from a carpenter or woodworking shop and a bottle of glue, create a sculpture of your own creative design.

Super Sculpture. Ahead of time, collect any kind of cardboard or paper items, such as toilet paper or wrapping paper rolls, small boxes, styrofoam trays, construction paper, etc. and at least one grocery carton. On Day 1, glue together a huge and wonderful sculpture. On Day 2, paint it with lots of different tempera colors. This is a great outdoor project with friends or cousins.

Tree House or Fort. This is one of the greatest adventures for older boys and girls. Some adult supervision will be necessary for safety.

Tent or Teepee. Your tent may be as simple as a blanket over the clothesline or a sheet over the jungle gym. But if you live where trees are abundant, try gathering long sticks, stacking them like a teepee, and wrapping a sheet around the finished cone.

Fruit and Cheese Kabobs. Mom should put out a variety of chunked fruit and cheese cubes with wooden kabob skewers. Let children build their own kabobs. Serve with milk and crackers.

Banana Popsicles. Insert a popsicle stick in the bottom half of a banana. Dip the banana in yogurt, then roll in crushed peanuts. Freeze for a healthy and delicious treat.

Ants on a Log. Start with a chunk of celery (the log). Fill with cream cheese, then set raisins (ants) all along the log.

Shape Sandwich. Cut bread, bologna, and cheese slices with a large cookie cutter. Stack them up to build your own shape sandwich. Don't forget to eat the scraps!

Summer Salad. From a selection of greens and vegetables, start with lettuce and build a summer salad. Add your family's favorite dressing. For protein, include small pieces of summer sausage, hard-boiled egg, cheese, or seeds. Raisins add sweetness and nourishment.

Peewee Pizzas. Spread pizza or spaghetti sauce on one half of an English muffin. Add grated cheese (or a slice) and chopped up summer sausage (or hot dog). Toast under the broiler in a toaster oven.

Veggie Pizza. Provide each child with a ready-made tube biscuit. Have the children flatten out the dough for a thin crust and then bake it. Spread dip on the crust. Children choose from dishes of finely chopped celery, carrot, zucchini, radishes, etc. to combine their own Veggie Pizza.

Apple Dessert. Core an apple and slice into medium thick circles. Lay a slice of cheese over the apple. Sprinkle lightly with sugar and cinnamon. Broil until cheese melts.

Nuts and Bolts. Use pretzel sticks (bolts) and Cheerios (nuts). Slip cheerio nuts onto pretzel bolts, then dip and eat. Or just crunch them as is.

Pocket Sandwich. Cut pita pocket bread in half. Each child can stuff his half with whatever Mom sets out:

shredded lettuce, grated cheese, chopped hard-boiled egg, browned hamburger, chopped summer sausage, raisins, crushed and dried pineapple, chopped veggies.

Summer Stories. Choose a day with some sunshine and lots of puffy clouds. Read the book *It Looked Like Spilt Milk* (see *Suggested Reading for Kids*). Go outdoors and lie down to see what you can imagine in the cloud formations. A whale in the ocean? Tell a story about a whale. Take turns seeing things and telling stories. Or, have each child look in a mirror and draw a picture of what he sees. Then he can write or tell a story about himself, including others in the adventure you make up.

Just for the Day

Your family could set aside an "Official ___ Day" for your family. Choose a theme for the day, then plan activities and meals around the theme.

Official Bear Day. Have porridge for breakfast (any hot, cooked cereal) and invite a teddy bear to join you at the table.

Read *We're Going on a Bear Hunt* (see *Suggested Reading for Kids),* then follow the steps in the book to do a "Bear Hunt."

Sing "Brown Bear" together (see *Suggested Reading for Kids).*

Read about real bears in a library book.

For lunch, make "Bears in a Cave." Wrap hot dogs in ready-to-bake crescent rolls and bake as directed. For dessert have teddy grahams.

Play the tape or record of "The Teddy Bear Picnic."

For supper, recreate a teddy-bear picnic. Take a bear along, choose a place near the woods, and be sure to include food that bears like to eat (tuna *fish* sandwiches, *honey* and peanut butter sandwiches, or *honey* graham crackers.

Have a Winnie-the-Pooh story or video for a bedtime story.

Official Baby Day. This is especially enjoyable if there is a new baby in the family or if one is expected.

Set up a sink or plastic tub for a baby bath. Using a child's doll, give everyone a how-to-bathe-a-baby lesson (how to support the head, not to use soap on the face, how to wrap in the towel). Point out all the accessories needed (baby soap, shampoo, towel and washcloth, powder, baby oil, diaper ointment, etc.). Include instructions on diapering. Let the children try it, using all the tools of the trade.

Fingerpaint in pink baby lotion.

Paint with pink and powder blue paints using Q-tips as brushes.

Let the children taste baby-food meat, vegetable, and custard.

Invite a friend who has a baby to join you, then sing "Hush, Little Baby" and "Rock-a-bye, Baby."

For a snack, have applesauce on graham crackers or Zwieback.

Read a Bible story about Hannah's special baby Samuel for a bedtime story.

Official Sand and Sun Day. If possible, go to the beach for the day. If this is not possible, a sandbox or a sandy play area at a playground will make it possible for you to do most of these activities.

Make a family sand sculpture together, or each one can mold what he wishes. The traditional castle is always creative, but you could try to mold your house or your church, your favorite animals, creatures from outer space, cars—there's no limit to the possibilities.

Do a Shadow Hop by making a shadow in the sun and then making moves to see if and how your shadow moves. Talk about what makes a shadow. Can you "shake" a shadow or make one disappear? Can you make it bigger or smaller?

Investigate evaporation. Early in the day put a clear plastic glass in the sun. Fill it with water and mark the water line. See how much water is absorbed into the air in one day.

Make sand pictures. Swirl glue on a paper just as if you were drawing a picture of the sea or life by the sea. Shake sand onto the glue.

Learn about flotation. Try floating in the water. If you know how, teach the children. On the beach or at home, fill two pails with water. Make a collection of objects (bringing some along will make the lesson more graphic). Study which things float and which don't as you drop them in the water. Try pennies, corks, nails, seashells, tree bark, pebbles, rubberbands, a spoon, a ball, sand, or feathers.

Official Windy Day. Choose a day with a really good wind outside! Have windy day fun by flying a kite or running with pinwheels.

Little children can make a "running kite." An older child can help cut a diamond or kite-shape piece of construction paper. The small child can decorate it with markers and staple on a crepe-paper streamer tail. Attach a five-foot piece of yarn. The small child can run with his kite out behind him on the wind.

For lunch, make kite sandwiches. Cut bread with a diamond-shaped cookie cutter. Cover with peanut butter, and attach a string-cheese tail.

Do outdoor explosion painting. Put blobs of tempera paint on a big sheet of paper. Lay on your stomach in front of the paper. Place one end of a straw in your mouth and the other end in front of the paint blobs. Blow hard! See what kind of painting your wind will create.

Study windworks. Talk about how men have harnessed the wind's energy to work for them—airplanes, hot air balloons, windmills, kites, and pinwheels.

Make indoor wind. Using a fan, show how wind can move objects (cotton, ribbon, pinwheels). Talk into the fan and listen to your voice as the sound waves are broken by the fan.

Have a cottonball race. Each participator has a straw and a cottonball. Choose a smooth floor, line the cottonballs in a row, and mark a finish line. The first to blow his cottonball to the finish line wins.

At the library, search out poems or stories about the wind.

For a bedtime story, read in Matthew about how Jesus calmed the wind and waves (or use a Bible storybook).

Official Noisy Day. Choose a day when you can finish up with a band concert in the park—or perhaps a day when there will be a parade through town.

Have someone play reveille first thing in the morning (in person or on tape) for a noisy wake-up call.

Have a noisy breakfast—Rice Krispies and milk!

Go on a Summer Sounds Walk (see page 197).

Read the "Country Noisy Book" (see *Suggested Reading for Kids).*

Have a crunchy lunch. No one should talk so that all can hear the "crunch" of celery and carrot sticks, potato chips, crackers with cheese, and apple slices for dessert.

For a noisy snack, put grapenuts or granola in your favorite flavor of yogurt. Eat it up before the "crunch" disappears.

Pack a picnic supper and attend a band concert under the stars.

End your Noisy Day with taps.

Suggested Reading for Kids

Young Readers

Aliki, *The Story of Johnny Appleseed; Hush, Little Baby; and We Are Best Friends.*

Asch, Frank, *Just Like Daddy.*

Bemelmans, Ludwig, the *Madeline* series.

Brown, Margaret Wise, *The Big, Red Barn; Country Noisy Book; Goodnight, Moon;* and *Home for a Bunny.*

Carle, Eric, *The Very Hungry Caterpillar.*

Crampton, Gertrude, *The Large and Growly Bear.*

de Paola, Tomie, *Mother Goose Rhymes; Charlie Needs a Cloak,* and others.

Eastman, P.D., *Are You My Mother?* and *The Best Nest.*

Fischer, Norma Bristol, *Who Could Love an Ugly Toad?*

Flack, Marjorie and Kurt Wiese, *The Story about Ping.*

Gospel Light, *Discovering Out of Doors* and *Discovering Little Things.*

Graham, Margaret Bloy, *Be Nice to Spiders.*

Gruelle, Johnny, *Raggedy Ann and Andy.*

Keats, Ezra Jack, *Whistle for Willie* and other stories.

Kraus, Robert, *Herman the Helper.*

Langstaff, John, *Over in the Meadow.*

LeBar, Mary, *How God Gives Us Ice Cream.*

Lobel, Arnold, *Frog and Toad Are Friends.*

Lowry, Janette Sebring, *The Poky Little Puppy* series.

Martin, Bill, Jr., *Brown Bear, Brown Bear, What Do You See?*

McLoskey, Robert, *Blueberries for Sal.*

Milne, A.A., *Winnie-the-Pooh* series.

Minarek, Else Holmelund, *Little Bear's Visit.*

Moncure, Jane Belk, *Thank You, God, for Summer.*
Parish, Peggy, *Amelia Bedelia.*
Piper, Watty, *The Little Engine That Could.*
Potter, Beatrix, *Peter Rabbit* and other stories.
Rey, Hana, The *Curious George* series.
Rosen, Michael, *We're Going on a Bear Hunt.*
Scarry, Richard, picture books.
Sendak, Maurice, *Chicken Soup with Rice.*
Sesame Street, *Sesame Street* books.
Shaw, Charles G., *It Looked Like Spilt Milk.*
Shely, Patrick, *Charlie's "Be Kind" Day.*
Speir, Peter, *Rain.*
Seuss, Dr., *The Cat in the Hat; Green Eggs and Ham,* et al.
Tudor, Tasha, *Five Senses.*
Wood, Audrey, *Quick as a Cricket.*
Zion, Gene, *The Summer Snowman; Harry by the Sea;* and
    other Harry stories.
Zolotow, Charlotte, *Big Sister and Little Sister.*

Middle Readers
Alcott, Louisa May, *Eight Cousins; Little Women.*
Baum, Frank L., *The Wizard of Oz.*
Burnett, Frances Hodgson, *The Secret Garden* and *A Little
    Princess.*
Cleary, Beverly, *Ramona the Pest; Runaway Ralph.*
Farley, Walter, *The Black Stallion.*
Fitzhugh, Louise, *Harriet the Spy.*
Grahame, Kenneth, *The Wind in the Willows.*
Konigsburg, Elaine, *From the Mixed-Up Files of Mrs. Basil
    E. Frankweiler.*
Knight, Eric, *Lassie Come Home.*
Longfellow, Henry Wadsworth, *Hiawatha.*
MacLachlan, Patricia, *Sarah, Plain and Tall.*
North, Sterling, *Rascal.*
Norton, Mary, *The Borrowers.*
de Saint-Exupery, Antoine, *The Little Prince.*
Sewall, Anna, *Black Beauty.*

Stevenson, Robert Louis, *Treasure Island.*
Travers, P.L., *Mary Poppins.*
White, E.B., *Charlotte's Web* and *Stuart Little.*
Wilder, Laura Ingalls, The *Little House* books.

Older Readers
Cleary, Beverly, *The Luckiest Girl.*
L'Engle, Madeleine, *Meet the Austins* and *A Wrinkle in Time.*
Lewis, C.S., *The Chronicles of Narnia.*
Little, Jean, *Look through My Window.*
MacDonald, George, *The Princess and the Goblin,* and modernized novels.
Montgomery, L.M., The *Anne of Green Gables* series.
O'Dell, Scott, *Island of the Blue Dolphins.*
Paterson, Katherine, *Jacob Have I Loved.*
Rawls, Wilson, *Where the Red Fern Grows.*
Taylor, Mildred, *Roll of Thunder, Hear My Cry* and *The Gold Cadillac.*
Tolkien, J.R.R., *The Hobbit.*
Twain, Mark, *The Adventures of Tom Sawyer.*
Verne, Jules, *Around the World in Eighty Days* and *20,000 Leagues Under the Sea.*

Suggested Reading for Parents

Campbell, Ross. *How to Really Love Your Child*. Wheaton, Ill.: Victor Books, 1960.

Christenson, Larry. *The Christian Family*. Minneapolis: Bethany House, 1970.

Dobson, James. *Hide or Seek*. Waco, Tex.: Word, 1987.

Dobson, James. *Parenting Isn't for Cowards*. Waco, Tex.: Word, 1987.

Dobson, James. *Preparing for Adolescence*. Ventura, Calif.: Regal Books, 1978.

Faber, Adele and Elaine Mazlish. *How to Talk So Kids Will Listen & Listen So Kids Will Talk*. New York: Avon Books, 1980.

Gore, Tipper. *Raising PG Kids in an X-rated Society*. Nashville: Abingdon Press, 1987.

Haystead, Wes. *Teaching Your Child About God*. Ventura, Calif.: Regal Books, 1981.

Lindskoog, John and Kathryn. *How to Grow a Young Reader*. Wheaton, Ill.: Shaw, 1989.

Mow, Anna B. *Preparing Your Child to Love God*. Grand Rapids, Mich.: Zondervan, 1983.

Murray, Andrew. *How to Raise Your Children For Christ*. Minneapolis: Bethany House, 1975.

Ortland, Anne. *Children Are Wet Cement*. Old Tappan, N.J.: Fleming H. Revell, 1981.

Peel, Kathy, and Joy Mahaffey. *A Mother's Manual for Summer Survival*. Waco, Tex.: Word, Inc., 1989.

Pelfrey, Wanda B. *Making the Most of Your Child's Teachable Moments*. Chicago: Moody Press, 1988.

Stanley, Charles. *How to Keep Your Kids on Your Team.* Nashville: Nelson Books, 1986.

Turecki, Stanley with Leslie Tonner. *The Difficult Child.* New York: Bantam Books, 1986.

Youth for Christ. *How to Raise Christian Kids in a Non-Christian World.* Wheaton, Ill.: Victor Books, 1988.

Index